x977.31
P51s
cop. 5

INTERIM SITE

Phelan, M
    The story of the great Chicago fire

450

Y0-CUZ-600

3 1192 00233 0502

1963

The Story of
THE GREAT
CHICAGO FIRE, 1871

The Story of
THE GREAT CHICAGO FIRE, 1871

BY MARY KAY PHELAN
Illustrated by William Plummer

Thomas Y. Crowell Company   New York

Copyright © 1971 by *Mary Kay Phelan*
Illustrations copyright © 1971 by
William Plummer
All rights reserved. Except for use in a review, the reproduction or utilization of this work in any form or by any electronic, mechanical, or other means, now known or hereafter invented, including xerography, photocopying, and recording, and in any information storage and retrieval system is forbidden without the written permission of the publisher. Published simultaneously in Canada by Fitzhenry & Whiteside Limited, Toronto

Designed by *Carole Fern Halpert*

Manufactured in the United States of America

L.C. Card 72-109910
ISBN 0-690-77671-3

1 2 3 4 5 6 7 8 9 10

Especially for

Lindsay Allison Phelan

who, I hope, will enjoy
delving into history as
much as I do!

By the Author

Four Days in Philadelphia—1776
Midnight Alarm: The Story of Paul Revere's Ride
Probing the Unknown:
The Story of Dr. Florence Sabin
The Story of the Great Chicago Fire, 1871

Acknowledgments

Much of the material in this book was found in original manuscripts, reminiscences, and personal letters deposited in the Chicago Historical Society. I wish to express my appreciation to the members of the society's library staff for their gracious assistance in helping me locate these materials and in checking the authenticity of certain facts.

I would also like to thank Congressman Fred Schwengel (First District, Iowa) for making arrangements for me to use all the facilities offered by the Library of Congress. The newspaper files for 1871 were particularly enlightening.

And I am most grateful to Hortense Finch, who made many helpful suggestions as the manuscript progressed; to my husband, Martin, and to our son, Jerry, whose enthusiasm for the Great Chicago Fire was a genuine source of inspiration.

Contents

1	Omen of Disaster	1
2	Saturday Night Spectacle	14
3	A Scream in the Night	25
4	From the O'Leary Barn . . .	37
5	Fire Spreads on the West Side	49
6	Peril for the South Side	59
7	The Flames Surge Northward	73
8	Red Tornado	85
9	North Side Holocaust	97
10	Out of Control	109
11	Continuing Calamity	122
12	Will It Never End?	134

13	*Smoking Ruins*	145
14	*"All Is Not Lost"*	157
15	*"Chicago Shall Rise Again"*	168
	Epilogue: 1875	177
	Bibliography	180
	Index	185

The Story of
THE GREAT CHICAGO FIRE, 1871

1

Omen of Disaster

In the gaslit auditorium of Farwell Hall the audience gasps in horror. On this Saturday night, October 7, 1871, the speaker is world-traveler and author George Francis Train. He has just finished a lengthy lecture with these words:

"This is the last public address that will be delivered within these walls! A terrible calamity is impending over the city of Chicago! More I cannot say; more I dare not utter."

The people in the audience turn to each other in bewilderment. What in the world is this man talking about? How can he possibly say such a thing? The more rational listeners realize that Mr. Train's pronouncement of doom has probably been only a trick, a speech-making tactic to electrify a group that has become somewhat restless in the stuffy auditorium. This fourth largest city in the nation—the Garden City, the Queen City of the West—about to face a terrible disaster? Impossible!

The people in Farwell Hall tonight, like most Chicagoans, are proud of the progress their city has made in the past thirty-eight years. It was a mere trading post with less than one hundred people when the city was formally organized in 1833. Expanding with incredible speed, far beyond anyone's expectation, Chicago in this year of 1871 boasts a population of more than 330,000 residents.

Situated on a low-lying flat plain, the city stretches six miles from north to south along Lake Michigan and has spread more than three miles west. Through this area flows the muddy Chicago River, forking into two branches about half a mile west of the lake, much like the letter T. One branch goes south and the other northwest, separating Chicago into three parts—officially known as divisions. More often they are called the North Side, the South Side, and the West Side.

CHICAGO 1871
The extent of the fire damage

Many of the early settlers made their homes on the North Side, and it is still primarily a residential area. Although Chicago gentlemen follow the creed of "everything at high pressure" in their business lives, they like to create in their home surroundings much of the atmosphere of the New England communities they left behind.

Large frame homes on the North Side are set amid spacious lawns. The residents here take pride in their gracious gardens and wide-spreading shade trees. They approve of the Latin motto on the city's seal, *Urbs in Horto,* which they happily translate as "the Garden City."

The main business district is concentrated in the South Side—that area bounded on the north by the

Chicago River and on the west by the river fork that meanders lazily southward. Here are all the fine retail stores, the wholesale establishments, public buildings and hotels, newspaper offices, theaters, churches, and the two great Union Railroad depots. In essence, the South Side is the heart of Chicago, where practically everything under the sun is bought and sold, where people work, play, and worship.

The city is still too young, however, to be solidly built up. Even downtown there are many vacant lots where weeds grow wild and trees abound. Often one- or two-story frame buildings are found next to the more pretentious "commercial palaces." In stark contrast to the South Side affluence is a small section near the river fork, easily recognized as the city's worst slum area. Thus, it is evident that in its fast-paced growth there has been little design or plan to the business district.

On the West Side is focused the city's industry, with its hundreds of factories, planing mills, distilleries, tanneries, and machine shops. Nestled alongside the industrial plants and sprawling out onto the prairie are the crowded frame dwellings where most of the laboring people live.

Getting from one part of the city to another poses few problems, since there is a series of wooden bridges

Omen of Disaster

that span the river and its forks at approximately two-block intervals. The bridges provide both roadways and pedestrian walks. In order to accommodate river traffic, however, each bridge rests on a fixed pier in the middle and is constructed to swing sideways whenever ships want to pass.

The most influential person in directing this traffic is the bridge tender. From the pier he operates the controls of the steam engine that turns the bridge. However, there are times when long lines of horsecars, wagons, drays, and pedestrians are forced to wait while a barge hauls its cargo upstream. Then, often as not, the poor man becomes the object of vicious insults.

More recently, however, the congestion of traffic has been somewhat relieved. Several years ago railroad king William B. Ogden declared he was tired of the "horrors of bridging" and financed construction of the Washington Street Tunnel under the south branch of the river. Its double roadway for vehicles and twelve-foot passage for pedestrians have been a real boon these past two years. Just last month a much larger tunnel was completed under the main river, leading off from LaSalle Street. Travel between the North and South sides does not try one's patience as it once did.

That Chicago is a city of wood cannot be denied. From the dense forests in northern Michigan and Wisconsin has come the pine that is both cheap and plentiful. It is much lighter to work with than brick, stone, or iron. And in their haste to expand, most people have chosen the easy mode of construction. Thousands and thousands of homes, factories, and retail stores have been built of this abundant pine, though the more imaginative will try to disguise the wood by painting or carving it to resemble stone.

For some of the newer downtown buildings, "Athens marble" has been used. It can be handsomely polished and presents a majestic front to the outside world. In reality, though, the "marble" is a medium-grade limestone, quarried at nearby Joliet, Illinois, and easily transported into the city. There is a current decorative trend—just imported from the East—to use cast-iron columns on the face of a building. But this is still so recent that only a few of the finest establishments can boast of it.

Mud has long been one of Chicago's biggest problems. Located as it is on a low-lying plain, the city has never had any system of drainage. Business buildings began sinking into the swampy land; roadways became seas of muck in wet weather. And during the dry season the city would be almost enveloped by swirling clouds of dust.

Omen of Disaster

A number of years ago various plans were suggested to defeat the mud. However, nothing was successful until the city government decided to build an entirely new surface. Dirt was hauled into the downtown area, and some streets were raised as much as ten feet in a project that required twenty years to complete.

But as the streets went up, the buildings appeared to sink farther down. It was during the late 1850's that a young Yankee cabinetmaker, George M. Pullman, arrived on the scene. (By this year, 1871, he is already famous for his invention of the railroad sleeping car.) Pullman had heard about Chicago's problem while he was helping move buildings during the widening of the Erie Canal. The ingenious young man was determined that something could be done for Chicago. With the help of two contractors, he undertook the job of raising an entire block of stores along Lake Street.

Six thousand jackscrews were placed under the buildings, and six hundred men hired to do the job. Each man was assigned ten screws and, at the proper signal, turned each of his screws a fraction of an inch. As the block rose slowly into the air, it was shored up with timbers. In four days the buildings were raised four feet without any interruption of business. When the new foundations were ready, the entire block was lowered in the same gentle manner. A year later, in 1861, Pullman contracted to elevate the city's largest hotel, the Tremont House. Not a teacup rattled, not a window pane cracked. Few of the guests ever knew that anything unusual was taking place.

There has been an effort to pave some of the city's 534 miles of streets. But, so far, not too much progress has been noted outside of the downtown area. A few of the streets have been covered with cobblestones or macadam, but fifty-five miles in the business district are paved with pine blocks, three inches square and six inches deep—Nicholson blocks, they are called. These blocks are laid on hemlock planks, fitted together like bricks, and tarred with a gravel surface. Eventually this surface is ground into the soft pine or swept away by the wind.

Sidewalks are almost exclusively made of pine planks and raised on wooden supports several feet above the ground. All streets, however, are not the same height, and thus the sidewalks are very irregular. Walking can be a dangerous exercise, stepping up two feet on one street and down three feet on another. Bruises, sprains, and broken bones are not uncommon, particularly in winter.

Much of Chicago's growth today may be attributed

to the first settlers, who set up their trading post, Fort Dearborn, on the western shore of Lake Michigan. Whether their choice of a site was sheer luck or good planning, no one really knows. Yet they could not have selected a more strategic location.

Before the coming of the railroads the Great Lakes formed the natural highway to the West. Almost everything came into Chicago by water. Barges, canal boats, steamers, and great sailing schooners deposited their cargoes on the thirteen miles of wooden docks and piers along the Chicago River. Huge grain elevators of wood and brick sprang up here, and now the city is capable of storing twelve million bushels of grain.

The ease of water transportation has been a boon to the lumber industry, too. From the north come tremendous loads of raw lumber. As a result there are many sawmills and woodworking factories scattered along the river or on nearby streets.

However, the water traffic has now been overshadowed by rail transportation. It was just twenty-three years ago—in the fall of 1848—that the Galena and Chicago Union Railroad opened the first line. And it was on this railroad, running west for ten miles, that the initial load of freight was brought into town.

Throughout the 1850's more and more railroads

laid tracks into the fast-expanding commercial center. Two years ago the Union Pacific completed its line to San Francisco, giving Chicago a direct route to the West Coast. Today there is an average of 100 passenger trains and 120 freight trains coming in or going out daily. Thus the city has become the hub of rail traffic to all parts of the country.

It is possible that Mr. Train's dire prediction in Farwell Hall tonight is based on the fact that during this past summer a great drought has gripped the Middle West. Wide rivers have shrunk to mere streams; brooks and water holes have dried up and become gullies of parched earth. Out on the ranges livestock have died of thirst, prairie fires raged out of control.

For Chicago, summer has been a long and merciless season, with the heat holding week after week. Between July and October less than three inches of rain have fallen, and this, mere sprinkles that evaporated almost before they reached the ground.

People say it has been the worst summer they can remember. By August the once-green lawns were already faded to a depressing tan shade. Leaves on the trees were withered and brown, dropping prematurely, skittering along the roadways, piling up in clusters beneath the wooden sidewalks. Around town, paint on the frame buildings has blistered badly. Shingles on the roofs have been warped by the sun; tar-paper coverings are beginning to curl. And always there has been wind—searing blasts of hot air sweeping in off the baked prairies, making the sweltering Chicagoans even more uncomfortable.

Everything is as dry as tinder—factories and homes, wooden pavements and plank sidewalks. Yet the people of Chicago are, for the most part, taking the weather in stride. These last few days have been particularly bad ones for fires—more than thirty alarms in less than a week. Still, no one has thought too much about it. Fires have become such a commonplace occurrence that people say they are inevitable.

Despite this casual attitude, however, the *Chicago Tribune* just last September 10 issued an ominous warning: "Chicago is a city of everlasting pine, shingles, sham, veneers, stucco, and putty. It has miles of fire-traps, pleasing to the eye, looking substantial, but all sham and shingles."

Nevertheless, Chicagoans believe themselves well protected by the impressive new water works on the North Side, an engineering marvel completed just four years ago. Before the water works was constructed, the city's water had been supplied from unreliable wells and the grease-choked Chicago River. Newspapers enjoyed chiding the city fathers by reporting that "a four-

inch fish made its appearance through an office hydrant" or that "thousands of minnows have been found in Chicago water pipes this winter."

After much pressure, the Common Council agreed to construct a system whereby fresh water would be drawn through a tunnel under the bed of Lake Michigan. Once the new water works was completed, everyone marveled at the unaccustomed purity of the water. A contemporary author, Franc B. Wilkie, writes, "The cleansing properties of the new water are wonderful. Children whose faces have been washed in it have been lost and never found. Their mothers cannot recognize them."

The pumping station and the high-rising water tower on Chicago Avenue near the lake are reassurance enough of the city's readiness in case of fire. The one-hundred-foot tower is an imposing monument in medieval style, complete with artificial turrets and ornamental battlements reminiscent of ancient European fortresses. Its very strength is symbolic of Chicago's new vigor. And there are many who feel that with the new pumping station, all the water in Lake Michigan will be available at a moment's notice.

2

Saturday Night Spectacle

As the audience files out of Farwell Hall tonight, there are many who notice a brilliant red glow illuminating the sky out on the West Side. The more apprehensive begin to wonder if this can possibly be the calamity that the lecturer has just predicted. But common sense tells them it is only another fire—of which there have been so many these past few months.

There is really nothing to be alarmed about: Chicago has a fine professional fire department. If the city were still manned by volunteer fire companies, there might be cause for worry. There was a time when competition among the volunteer companies was so intense that the men were more interested in fighting each other than in putting out the blaze. Too often, if rival companies arrived at the scene of a fire, a hand-to-hand battle was waged "for the honor of saving the property." By the time the combat ended, there was usually nothing left to save.

All that changed, however, in 1858, when the Chicago Fire Department became a professional organization. It is now administered by three elected commissioners known as the Board of Police. These men are responsible for both the Fire and Police departments of the city; funds to support the departments come from taxes and are appropriated by the Common Council. The board often complains that the council tries to economize too much, particularly when it comes to equipment for the Fire Department.

However, by comparison with other communities, Chicago's equipment is quite up-to-date. There are seventeen steam-driven fire engines, which have replaced the cumbersome hand-pumped models. A steamer makes an impressive appearance with its shiny brass-plated boiler and fittings mounted on a four-wheel carriage, drawn by a team of four horses. Each steamer has a departmental number, but more often it is known by a name, such as *Winnebago* or *Waubansia,* after the Indian tribes. Other steamers have taken names of famous politicians. The *Long John* honors a former mayor, John Wentworth; and the *Little Giant* is the affectionate nickname for Stephen A. Douglas.

In addition to the steamers there are twenty-three hose carts, four hook-and-ladder wagons, and two hose elevators. The hose elevator has a platform that can be lifted about two stories high. From the platform the fireman directs a stream of water to the upper floors of a building. However, the hose elevators have not been too successful—one is already out of order. Most of the fire fighting is done at ground level.

The 48,000 feet of hose that belongs to the Fire Department often presents problems. Most of the hose is rubber—of rather poor quality—and is prone to burst when overloaded. There are still some leather hoses used, although during the winter months the leather freezes and the department is left in short supply. Just last month an additional 15,000 feet was requested, but the penny-pinching council has not yet seen fit to authorize the purchase.

The Fire Department is staffed by a chief marshal, three assistants, and 185 active firemen. The firemen are on duty around the clock, with time out for meals and an occasional day off. Most of the officers and men

Saturday Night Spectacle

are brawny, strapping daredevils who sport luxuriant beards and mustaches. They are fearless fighters, many being veterans of the Civil War. Pay is unusually good for these times and morale is high, since the officers of the department are almost always chosen from the ranks.

Very reassuring to Chicagoans is the fire-alarm telegraph system now in use. Wires have been stretched over housetops throughout the city, and alarm boxes placed at frequent intervals. Any citizen spotting a fire can run to the nearest box and turn in a signal. This is instantly recorded in the central office on the upper floor of the courthouse. The operator on duty then relays this signal to the nearest engine house, where horses are standing harnessed day and night, ready to speed the steam engine to the fire.

Formerly these alarm boxes were made of wood and operated by a hand crank that was, more often than not, out of order. However, just last month the city completed a much-needed renovation by replacing the wooden boxes with sturdy iron containers, operated by a single pull-down lever. Because of the increasing number of false alarms that have been turned in, the new boxes are kept locked and the keys given to responsible individuals in nearby houses or stores.

Furthermore, there is a watchman on duty atop each

engine house from 9:30 P.M. to 6:30 A.M.—the hours of greatest potential danger. Because the courthouse commands the best view of the entire area, a watchman is also stationed there, day and night, checking on the city through his spyglass. Should he sight a fire, he estimates its location and calls down the speaking tube to the central office, advising what signal should be rung. These carefully planned methods of alarm are a great satisfaction to those who worry about fires.

Just five days ago something brand-new was added to the forces for fire protection—the Insurance Patrol. It is the brainchild of Benjamin Bullwinkle, who was a former driver for the chief marshal. The patrol, supported by merchants and insurance companies, roams through the business district with chemical fire extinguishers mounted on a wagon. They can put out small fires and prevent the spread of sparks from burning buildings.

Yes, most Chicagoans feel themselves well guarded against fire hazards. Only those close to the Fire Department know that the board and the chief marshal have been pleading with the Common Council to install larger water mains. There has been an urgent request for at least two fireboats to guard the river. And proposal after proposal has been made for stricter ordinances that will regulate building codes. But there seems to be neither money for the equipment nor the inclination to enforce safety construction.

The glow now lighting the sky in the southern part of the West Side has resulted from a fire that started in the boiler room of the Lull and Holmes planing mill on Canal Street, near Van Buren. Before firemen could reach the scene flames devoured the mill, and they are now licking their way northward, fanned by a fourteen-mile-an-hour breeze.

The *Little Giant* has already arrived and is pumping water on the spreading blaze. But the neighboring lumberyard, vinegar works, paper-box factory, and cheap frame houses are only adding fuel to the fire. This is the area known to insurance men as "The Red Flash"—for reasons that are obvious to the most casual observer.

Matthias Benner, an assistant marshal, surveys the situation and decides to send in a second alarm. At present only equipment from the immediate area is here. The second alarm brings engines from farther away. It also brings John Schank and Lorens Walters, the other two assistants, as well as Chief Marshal Robert A. Williams.

Williams, a native of Canada, came to Chicago

when he was twenty-two years old and joined the volunteer fire department the following year. He has risen through the ranks until now, at the age of forty-five, he holds the top spot in his profession.

Williams is a powerfully-built man, more than six feet tall. His black hair is only slightly tinged with gray and his ruddy face has few lines to show for all the problems of his responsible position. Like many men today, he wears a mustache and spade beard, which cause people to remark that he bears a striking resemblance to General Robert E. Lee. His official uniform is a long, belted rubber coat with brass buttons, a heavy helmet, and a brass speaking trumpet carried in his right hand. The trumpet is essential, since this is often the only way to communicate with the men above the roar of a fire. The arrival of Robert Williams never fails to cheer his men; his very presence inspires confidence.

Quickly sizing up the progress of the fire, Chief Williams turns in a third alarm. This one will bring out all the equipment the city owns. Surround the fire with all the equipment available, he orders, and pour water on anything that is burning or threatened.

As the wind shifts to the southwest, more and more buildings are caught up in the fury of the spreading flames. People living in the miserable frame shanties

are following their usual practice of carrying their furniture out into the middle of the street, then fleeing on foot, with the hope that by some miracle their household goods will be saved. But such strategy only serves as a bridge for the fire to leap from one side of the street to the other, destroying everything in its path.

Buildings are now collapsing all around, sending out wide sheets of sparks. In less than twenty minutes the area between Jackson, Adams, and Clinton streets and the river is alive with flames. Like any fire, this blaze has drawn a large crowd of spectators—it's great Saturday night entertainment. Some watch from the safety of the bridge approaches, but others crowd closer, clogging the streets and hampering the fire fighters. The police are trying to push back the crowds, though they have little success.

Every available piece of equipment in the city is at the scene. Firemen are fighting desperately but they need more hands, so Chief Williams presses citizen volunteers into service. This is not unusual, since the department is still understaffed, and volunteers are expected to take part during a big fire.

It appears that the passenger cars on the Pittsburgh, Fort Wayne, and Chicago tracks will soon go up in flames. The chief wants to know if the volunteers can't do something. They can—and do. In spite of searing heat, the citizens tear down a wooden shed and manage to move the passenger cars down the track away from the oncoming flames.

Saturday Night Spectacle

Over on the northwest corner of Adams and Canal streets Daniel W. Quirk suddenly realizes that his tavern will be in the direct path of the fire if it sweeps across Adams Street. Acting on a generous impulse, Mr. Quirk decides to hand out free drinks and cigars to everyone in the little wooden tavern—so sure is he that the building will catch fire anyway. Quirk then hurries off to save his personal belongings.

The grateful patrons decide to try to save the building. Snatching up buckets, they rush to the river bank and return to throw water on the smoking walls. Their efforts pay off. Not only is Mr. Quirk's place of business saved, but the fire is prevented from getting a foothold on the entire block.

Despite the blinding smoke the firemen are fighting, inch by inch, for an advantage. While onlookers at a comfortable distance shrink away from the leaping flames, the firemen stand their ground within a dozen feet of the blaze. Occasionally they must retreat to catch a breath of air, but within seconds they are back, fighting with more determination than ever.

Not until 3:30 A.M. is the fire finally brought under control. It has been a long and terrifying struggle. Four blocks are burned out almost completely, despite the heroic efforts of the firemen. Only one commercial building still stands in the smoldering area, and that in itself is a mystery. The huge wooden National Elevator beside the river has only been scorched. No one can understand how it could possibly have withstood the worst conflagration the city has ever experienced.

In addition to all the destruction, the fire has taken a heavy toll of the department's equipment. A hose cart has been completely destroyed and the *William James* engine has been seriously damaged. Since the *Liberty* is already in the shop for repairs, this leaves only fifteen available engines for the city's protection.

After such a frightful siege, the firemen are exhausted. Their clothes are burned, their faces scorched, their eyelids red and swollen from the stinging cinders. Many are almost ready to collapse, and the chief sends them home to recuperate. In a check of available manpower, Williams finds there are only 125 firemen still fit for duty, and they need rest badly.

Just before dawn the chief marshal goes home for breakfast, leaving assistant Benner in charge. All that is left to do now is to keep pouring water on a few small fires still smoldering in the burned-out area. Williams is fervently hoping there will not be another alarm before his men and equipment are all back in service.

3

A Scream in the Night

An uneasy stillness has settled over the city on this Sunday morning, October 8, 1871. The day dawns clear and bright, although the early morning temperature of 51 degrees seems even cooler because of southerly breezes blowing in at nineteen miles an hour. Over on the West Side the only fire that remains is in a large pile of coal, still blazing with a bluish flame and throwing out clouds of smoke that streak the sky.

At 7:45 A.M. the United States Weather Bureau Office issues the following forecast: "The barometer will probably fall, with increasing southerly winds and rising temperatures, followed by cloudy or threatening weather during the night." This is good news to everyone—perhaps at last there will be some welcome rain.

Sunday is always a peaceful day in Chicago; all activity ceases and many residents make their way to one of the city's sixty-five churches. In addition to attending religious services, they also have ample time for leafing through the newspapers. And today's stories hold more interest than usual. Last night's blaze on the West Side is the *Chicago Tribune*'s lead article: "The Fire Fiend: A Terribly Destructive Conflagration."

The reporter gives a graphic account, detailing the progress of the fire hour by hour. Estimated losses total more than $750,000. It is very probable, however, that few readers give much heed to the last paragraph, in which the writer states:

> For days past, alarm has followed alarm, but the comparatively trifling losses have familiarized us to the pealing of the Court House bell, and we had forgotten that the absence of rain for three weeks had left everything in so dry and inflammable a condition that a spark might start a fire which would sweep from end to end of the city.

Equally shocking in today's *Tribune* is the full account of the wanton murder of a prominent merchant, Barton Edsall, last Thursday night. Edsall was shot to death in the front hall of his luxurious Washington Square home. The motive still remains a mystery, although the reporter probes all the angles, making good reading for the curious.

Even the ads are tinged with scare headlines. "Fire! Fire!" proclaims the Mutual Security Insurance Company as the copy urges prospective applicants to take out policies against the probable fall and winter fires.

There is welcome relief, however, in the Sunday supplement of the *Tribune.* A brand-new piece by that popular short-story writer, Bret Harte, is printed in full. Most people agree that "The Outcasts of Poker Flat" is "a corker."

The past summer has been fairly quiet. But now everyone is back in town and ready for the winter's activities. The fall theatrical season opens tomorrow night with an important "first night" at Chicago's most fashionable playhouse, the Hooley Theatre on Randolph Street. Mrs. F. W. Lander will play the title role in *Elizabeth,* with James H. Taylor as Essex.

It has become a favorite pastime among visitors from the East to complain that Chicago is a vulgar town. It has grown too fast, say its critics. There is too much emphasis on making money. Flimsy and gaudy construction characterize its architecture. The thriving community is like a greedy octopus, always reaching for more. What the critics do not realize is that behind all this hustle and haste is a spirit of enterprise and originality which does not appear at first glance.

There are, of course, those prophets of doom who declare that Chicago has become a city of sin, with gambling palaces and saloons outnumbering the grocery stores—"the wickedest place on earth." Most people, though, only laugh at such assertions and point with pride to the city's sixty-five private schools and colleges, its six medical schools, and its many cultural advantages.

Citizens here are known to be more widely read than those of any other community. Evidence of this fact is proven by the prosperity of Booksellers' Row. Along State Street the five-story marble-front buildings are filled with books of impressive quality, eagerly purchased by thousands of customers.

The gallery at the Academy of Design farther south on State Street displays more than three hundred paintings by American and European artists. The Academy of Sciences houses the Audubon Club's collection of game birds and mammals as well as extensive quantities of rare insects, marine shells, minerals, and a herbarium with 6,000 species of plants. Wood's Museum, not to be outdone, advertises that it has "the largest collection of curiosities in the West," including a ninety-six-foot fossil called Zeuglodon, a sea lion, a lighted panorama of London, and a hall of paintings.

A North Side addition to the city's cultural life is the new building for the Chicago Historical Society. Constructed of brick and stone, it is situated on the northwest corner of Dearborn and Ontario streets. At the dedication just three years ago the building was said to be "spacious and perfectly fireproof." In addition to the 18,000-volume library, the society has collected much of value about the early history of the city. There are large reading and lecture rooms and a public reception hall, where daily newspapers are available to everyone.

The most prized possession of the Historical Society is the perfect draft of President Lincoln's Emancipation Proclamation. In 1863 Chicago held its first Sanitary Fair—a charity benefit to aid the wounded Civil War soldiers. The President was persuaded to contribute for auction the draft of the proclamation, which he had laboriously copied for final approval by his cabinet. There is some evidence that it was "with great reluctance" that Mr. Lincoln parted with this manuscript.

The proclamation brought $3,000 at the auction, the greatest amount of money for any individual gift. The purchaser, Thomas B. Bryan, in turn presented the precious document to the Soldiers' Home. However, the trustees of the Home decided to place the manuscript in the Chicago Historical Society's new fireproof building for safekeeping. The document has been mounted in a locked glass case on the wall of the reception hall for everyone to see and admire.

For the more sports-minded enthusiasts in Chicago, there is the comparatively new game of baseball. Chicago's team, the White Stockings, plays in a wooden ball park on the lake front between Randolph and Washington streets. It is practicing daily for next Thursday's game with the Haymakers of Troy, New York. The first professional baseball league, the National Association, was formed at the beginning of this 1871 season, and there is a good chance that the White Stockings may win the championship. Today's paper notes that "a capacity crowd is expected."

As the day wears on, the temperature begins to soar. By 2:00 P.M. it is 85 degrees and there is a stiff

A Scream in the Night

breeze recorded at thirty-five miles an hour. Neither the heat nor the wind keeps the hundreds of sightseers away from the West Side. The streets are alive with traffic. All afternoon there is the clop of hoofs, the rattle of hansom cabs and elegant carriages. Horsecars are crowded with the curious—everyone wants to see last night's destruction.

About three o'clock Chief Marshal Williams begins making the rounds of the engine houses. He wants to be sure that the men, the horses, and the equipment are being well cared for after the all-night struggle.

At dusk Williams shows up at the scene of the fire. The pungent odor of burned wood and soggy ashes is still rising from the ruins. Occasionally a puff of smoke bursts upward from embers buried deep in the debris, but for all practical purposes the fire is out.

Satisfied, the chief returns to his official wagon and heads for home. Bumping over the pine-block paving, he sees youths hurrying from one corner to the next, lighting the gas street lamps. It is still warm, but fortunately the wind has died down. Williams reflects that his wife is probably preparing supper before going to the Sunday-night church service. He decides that just this once he will try to get some rest, rather than accompany her.

Although there are many who do attend the evening services, the proprietor of Crosby's Opera House on Washington Street has other plans. The Opera House has been closed all summer and $80,000 has been expended on redecorating. Installation of the carpeting and upholstery, woven in France to Crosby's specifications, was completed yesterday. Now that it is dark, he wants to see the effect of his renovation as it will appear when illumined by gaslight.

Everything must be in readiness for tomorrow night. Mr. Crosby cannot help but recall how the original opening of the Opera House in 1865 was delayed by the assassination of President Lincoln. But of course nothing like that will ever happen again. An ambitious symphonic orchestra season is scheduled, with Theodore Thomas conducting. The first concert is a sellout; the advance ticket sale for this fall series indicates there will be record attendance. The *Chicago Tribune* critic has predicted "an evening memorable both in sight and sound."

Out on the West Side this evening it is unusually quiet, in contrast to the roar and excitement of last night's fire. Several blocks south of the flame-ravaged area live most of the city's Irish and Scandinavian families. Sturdy, hard-working, and independent, these people are the laborers in the neighboring lumberyards, mills, and small factories.

Their tiny frame dwellings, one or two stories high, are fitted onto narrow lots about twenty-five feet wide. Some of the houses are built directly on the ground, while others are elevated a few feet and rest on cedar posts. The lots, often separated by high wooden fences, run back to a depth of about one hundred feet, leaving ample room for the necessary barns and sheds. Unpaved alleys, parallel to the streets, divide the blocks in half.

Now that winter is coming, every house in the area is well stocked with waste materials from the nearby woodworking mills. The shavings and lumber ends make an ideal fuel for both heating and cooking stoves. The provident householders have stored their supplies in sheds, yards, or the convenient open spaces under the houses. No matter how low the temperature falls, these people are ready for the cold weather ahead.

The property at No. 137 on the north side of DeKoven Street belongs to a laborer, Patrick O'Leary. He bought it seven years ago, in 1864, for only $500 and has been living here with his family since 1866. On the premises stand two small frame dwellings. The cottage fronting on DeKoven is rented to Mr. and Mrs. Patrick McLaughlin. McLaughlin, a railroad worker, never fails to pay his rent on time—something the owner appreciates.

The O'Learys with their five children occupy the shingled cottage a few feet behind the McLaughlins. At the back of the lot is a peaked-roof barn in which are kept five cows, a calf, a horse, and a small wagon.

Kate O'Leary, a stocky woman of thirty-five, has a small dairy business in order to supplement Mr. O'Leary's meager wages. She peddles fresh milk in the neighborhood. Just this afternoon the winter's food supply for the livestock has been delivered. Now there is a two-ton load of timothy hay stored in the loft. It is gratifying to Kate to know that her animals will not go hungry this winter.

Across the street from the O'Learys' property lives Danny Sullivan, a drayman, who answers to the nickname of "Peg-leg," for obvious reasons. About eight o'clock tonight Sullivan decides to wander over to the O'Learys' home. Limping across the street, he knocks on the little pine door, only to be greeted by a sleepy-eyed Patrick O'Leary. Everyone is in bed, says the Irishman, so Peg-leg takes the hint and stays just long enough to ask whether the O'Learys have seen the ruins from last night's fire.

Sauntering slowly back across the road, Danny decides it's too warm an evening to go inside yet. He'll plop down on the wooden sidewalk for a while and enjoy the balmy air he knows will soon be replaced by cold winter winds. From the McLaughlins' front parlor come the sounds of a fiddler playing a sprightly polka. The McLaughlins are giving a party for Mrs. McLaughlin's "greenhorn brother," who has just arrived from Ireland. Danny can't help but envy their fun.

He pulls out a pocket watch and notes that it's now

8:30 P.M., time to turn in for the night. Slowly he hoists himself to a standing position, but just as he straightens up, a fearful sight catches his eye. A sudden thrust of flame is shooting out from the O'Learys' barn.

"Fire! Fire! Fire!"

Danny's screams pierce the quiet of DeKoven Street. And he dashes across the dirt road toward the barn as fast as his peg-leg will carry him.

4

From the O'Leary Barn...

Half running, half hobbling, Danny rushes along the narrow pathway leading to the barn. As he passes the O'Leary cottage, he sees that it's all dark. Everyone must be sound asleep, but there's no time now to awaken the family. He must try to save Kate's precious livestock—if it's not too late.

There is a glowing mist of fire flowing along the east side of the barn as Danny throws open the door. It's impossible to reach the horse and two cows tied on that side. But he moves quickly to loosen the ropes of the other two cows and a calf tethered on the west wall, trying to shove them out of the barn door. The panic-stricken cows will not budge. However, the lively little calf is easy to manage, and Danny tugs on her rope as he gropes his way toward the open door. Suddenly his wooden leg sinks between two floorboards and is jammed so tightly that he cannot move.

With admirable calmness he reaches down with one hand to unstrap the wedged limb, just as the whirling mist of fire explodes into sheets of flame. Still holding tightly to the calf's rope, he hops out of the doorway, dragging the animal behind him. Both are singed but not burned. The cow tied up outside the barn has already disappeared.

The sight of the flames and the sound of Danny's screams have aroused everyone in the neighborhood except the O'Learys. Dennis Rogan, who lives next door, dashes into the alley hoping to rescue Kate O'Leary's delivery wagon, but the heat drives him back. His next thought is for the sleeping family, and he runs up on their porch, pounding on the door. Patrick, only half awake, comes out "scratching his head as if there was a foot of lice in it." The sight of the smoking barn sends him back into the house, screaming for his wife and the children to get out.

Within a few moments the furious fire inside the

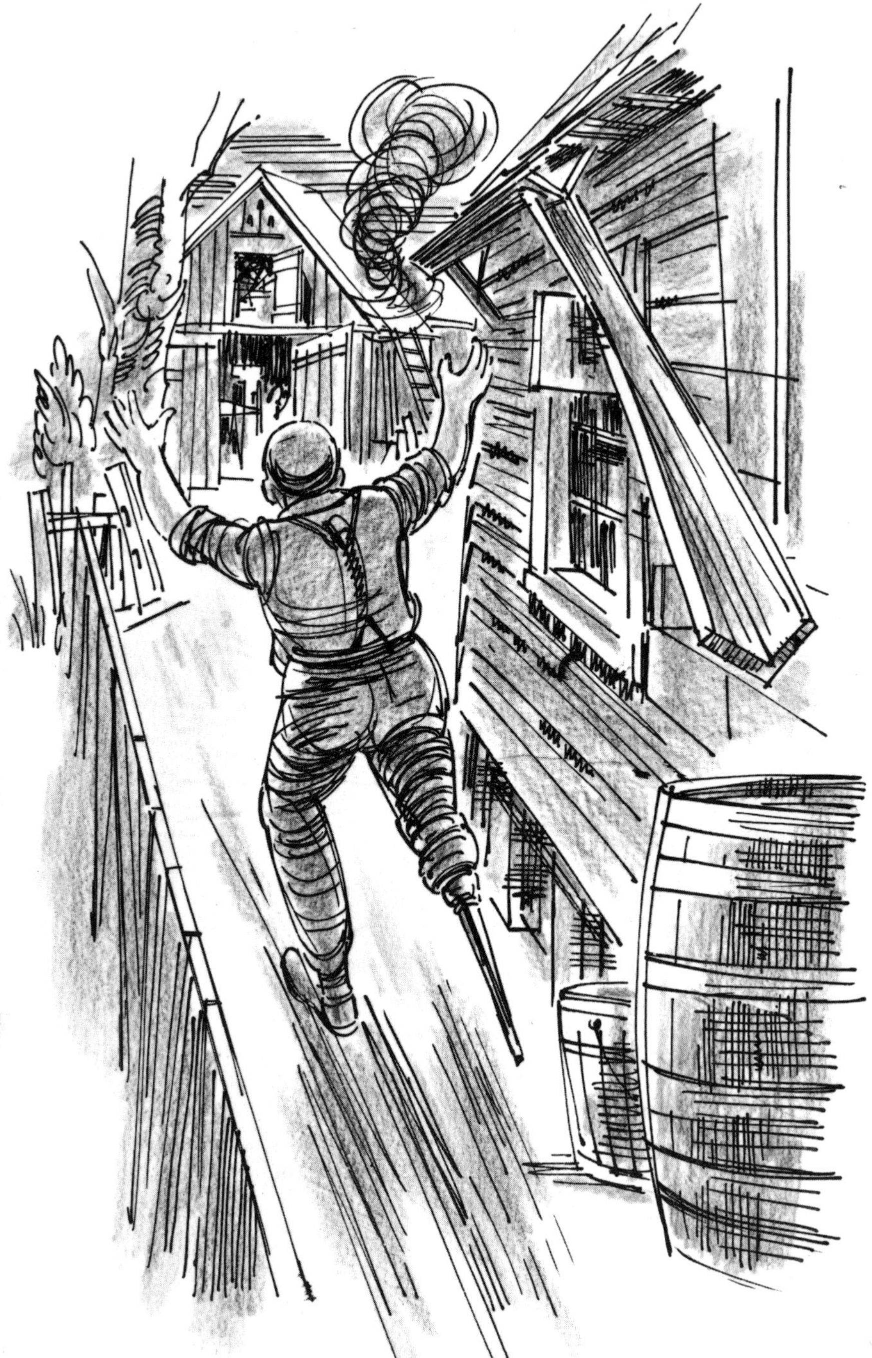

barn blows a jagged hole in the roof. Dense smoke billows upward in great clouds. The intense heat causes the wooden cottage to begin smoldering. O'Leary, with the help of several neighbors, forms a bucket brigade to throw water on his little home, while Kate clasps her hands and moans.

Two houses east of the O'Learys', William Lee is in his second-floor bedroom fastening the shutters when he sees flames spurting from the roof of the barn. He dashes downstairs, out the front door, and races three blocks south to Bruno Goll's drugstore at Canal and Twelfth streets, where the nearest alarm box has been installed.

Although the fire is now ten minutes old, Lee is the first person to have thought of turning in an alarm. Mr. Goll pulls down the lever, but for some unknown reason the signal does not register at the central fire headquarters in the courthouse. Ten minutes later another neighbor rushs into the store yelling "Fire! Fire!" For the second time Goll pulls down the lever. This alarm, too, is never received.

Meanwhile, over at the *Little Giant* engine house about six blocks south of DeKoven, the firemen have finished caring for their horses and cleaning their steamer. They are now in bed, and Joseph Lagger has

From the O'Leary Barn . . . 41

gone up to the lookout tower a little earlier than usual to begin his night-watch duty. He settles himself down in his chair and is struggling not to fall asleep when his attention is suddenly caught by a cloud of smoke rising swiftly above the rooftops.

"Turn out! Turn out!" he shouts down the winding stairway.

Exhausted though they are, the men are dressed and ready to go by the time Lagger runs down from the tower. The foreman signals headquarters that Company Six is rolling, and they clatter northward at a swift pace.

Flames leaping fifty feet into the air lead them directly to DeKoven and Jefferson streets, where the hose is attached and the line stretched down through the O'Leary yard. A steady stream of water is soon being sprayed on the burning barn from the hose of the *Little Giant,* the first steamer to reach tonight's fire. Within a few minutes the *Chicago* engine pulls up. The men have been alerted by a passerby, who stuck his head in the engine house and told them there was a blaze on DeKoven.

Up in the courthouse cupola Mathias Schafer, the watchman, has been chatting with a few visitors. They notice what they believe to be smoke out in the southwest, but Schafer tells them it's probably coming from the piles of burning coal left over from last night's fire. However, when the signal from *Little Giant*'s engine house comes in, Schafer takes a more careful look through his spyglass. Yes, he does see flames somewhere out on the West Side. That's odd—no alarms have been received. He'll have to estimate its location.

Watchman Schafer prides himself on the accuracy with which he makes his estimates, but tonight the West Side is blurred with smoke. He decides to place the fire at Canalport and Halsted, not knowing that his estimate is almost a mile southwest of the O'Leary barn. It is exactly 9:21 P.M. as the huge courthouse bell starts ringing the first alarm . . . 3-4-2. Almost forty minutes have elapsed since William Lee asked druggist Goll to signal central headquarters about the fire.

In his Randolph Street apartment on the South Side, Chief Robert Williams has fallen into an exhausted sleep. However, when the signal is given out from courthouse headquarters, it registers on instruments beside his bed and he awakens instantly. The chief is dressed and out of the apartment before the bell has stopped tolling. His official wagon comes roaring down the street, and the driver slows the horses

From the O'Leary Barn . . .

only enough to allow Williams to hop aboard. They are off across the Randolph Street bridge, speeding out toward the southwest. What in the world has happened, Williams wonders, to cause so much fire before an alarm has been sounded?

By the time the chief reaches the scene, three houses east of the O'Learys' are burning, as well as several barns and sheds. The heat of the flames is creating a strong draft, and sparks are being blown into nearby yards, setting fire to shavings and wood piles. But where are all the fire companies? Why haven't more steamers answered the alarm? What has happened?

Having battled thousands of fires, Robert Williams understands the characteristics and the surprises inherent in a roaring blaze. He can detect the underlying fierceness of smoke that is not apparent to someone with less experience. Now one swift glance is enough for Williams to know they will need more help, and he asks foreman Dorsey to turn in a second alarm.

With the arrival of more engines and men, the chief feels new confidence. The fire is still not out of control. However, he will have to stretch a thin line of defense around the burning area. Actually, he would much prefer to mass the equipment north of the fire and fight the oncoming flames directly, but he dares not leave the rear unprotected because the changeable wind may suddenly shift and whip the fire backward.

The steamer *Chicago* has been wetting down the opposite side of the street, and the firemen hope that the flames will not leap across. Then a breakdown appears in the hoses. One section bursts. Blankets are hastily tied around the breaks and held down with wooden planks—but the gesture is useless. The leaks are too frequent to allow any pressure to be maintained. Precious time is lost while the men search for hoses from another cart.

At this moment former alderman James H. Hildreth appears. He has heard the clatter of the engines speeding past his home at 574 Halsted Street and has come to give Chief Williams some advice. Hildreth believes it would be good strategy to blow up buildings that are in the path of the flames.

The harried Williams says that he has neither the power nor the powder to destroy other people's property. The meddling Hildreth persists, informing the chief that he knows where powder is available. "Go ahead and find it," says Williams, thinking perhaps that such an errand will keep Hildreth from bothering him further just now.

Williams is more worried about the wind than anything else. All day long strong gusts have been blowing in from the southwest. Shortly after dark the wind

From the O'Leary Barn . . . 45

died down, but now it seems to be increasing again. Flaming brands are being hurled high above the firemen's streams of water, carried out in a northeasterly direction. The chief only hopes that alert citizens will watch for these blazing torches to fall and will put them out before new fires spring up.

Now the flames have been raging for more than an hour. They have burned out one block and crossed over to another. Admittedly, it's a serious situation, but still not as critical as last night's destructive fire.

Up in the cupola on top of the courthouse Mathias

Schafer has been following the progress of the fire on the West Side through his spyglass. The sky is growing steadily brighter. Sparks are being blown across the river into the South Side. At times there almost seems to be a shower of "red snow." On his own initiative watchman Schafer decides to send out a third alarm. Certainly the chief will need everything available to control the spreading blaze.

People on the South Side have been awakened by the commotion of the fire engines clattering by. They peer out of their windows and are startled by the sight of the leaping flames across the river. Groups gather on the streets to talk about the destruction over in the West Side, but everyone is confident that by the time the flames reach the site of last night's fire there will be nothing to worry about. Those who have been attending evening church services find it difficult to make their way home in the face of the increasing gusts of wind.

Back at the O'Learys', the bucket brigade is still pouring water on the smoking house. It appears now that the O'Learys' little home has escaped destruction. In the face of what the neighbors have lost, O'Leary is grateful that it was only his barn that was swept away by the fire.

Meanwhile, the flames are licking their way along the north side of Taylor Street toward Canal. Williams dashes down the dirt road searching frantically for equipment to stop this fresh outbreak. The *Long John,* the *Waubansia,* and the *Titsworth* have arrived, and the chief directs them to pull out everything they have. "Get in close," he urges, "and hang on as long as you possibly can."

Over on the South Side Thomas Ockerby, night superintendent of the Gas Works, reported for duty at 5:30 this afternoon. Now, five hours later, he is alarmed by the constant shower of sparks from the West Side fire that seem to be landing near his plant in an endless stream. He decides to take some defensive action.

Calling in the assistant superintendent, Ockerby explains that he fears the fire may spread. If, by some remote chance, it should reach the Gas Works, there could be a terrible explosion. Together the men go into the plant and turn the valves so that all the gas in the tanks is transferred out of the South Side into the huge reservoirs located north of the river.

The fire on the West Side has now reached Canal Street. Both sides of the street are burning, and buildings two blocks north on Ewing Street are being devoured by the flames. With about a dozen steamers now at the scene, the chief splits them up in three groups. One is working at the original site, while the second is pouring water on fires that have spread north and west. The third group is massed north and east of the blaze.

With so little equipment, with men already exhausted from last night's ordeal, the lines of defense are much too thin. But the fire fighters are persistent. And now Chief Williams is beginning to hope that the flames can be stopped in the area around Ewing Street.

Precisely at 10:00 P.M. a blazing firebrand soars high into the air and is carried four blocks to the tower roof of St. Paul's Catholic Church at Clinton and Mather streets. Williams is startled when one of the men races up to tell him that St. Paul's is on fire. He can hardly believe it—why, that's two blocks behind him. If the flames get a start on this tall frame structure, masses of burning material will be scattered over a far greater area than he likes to imagine. It must be stopped!

5

Fire Spreads on the West Side

Chief Williams is upset by this sudden change of fate. He needs everything he has right here to keep the fire from spreading. However, if St. Paul's is burning, there's no choice. He shouts for George Rau, foreman of the hook-and-ladder wagon *Protection*. "Raise your longest ladder," directs the chief, adding that he will send an engine as quickly as possible. Fortunately, the *Coventry* and the *Rhem* are just turning into Taylor Street, and Williams waves them on toward St. Paul's.

By the time the steamers reach the church, the steeple has disappeared, the roof has burned off, and the flames are licking their way down the inside of the building. The saints and angels on the stained glass windows are vivid, almost alive, as the fire from within throws its flashing changes of color against the figures. Several firemen attempt to rescue the holy relics so dear to the St. Paul's communicants, but the searing heat drives them back.

Just behind the church are two huge four-story shingle mills belonging to W. B. Bateham. Mr. Bateham is a former fire marshal. As a prominent businessman in his later years, he has been elected alderman of the Ninth Ward. He arrived half an hour ago to see whether his mills were in danger. At first he thought the buildings were well away from the fire. However, after St. Paul's began burning, Bateham took quick action. Volunteers were enlisted to wet down the sides and roofs of the mills. As blazing pieces of wood from St. Paul's begin falling on the tarpaper roof of one of the mills, Bateham dashes up to the top himself and douses the small fires with feverish intensity.

Suddenly the walls of the great church collapse. The heavy beams come thundering down, sending out a billowing cloudburst of sparks. Violent winds catch the sparks, whirling them in every direction. Seeing the sudden danger created by the wind, Bateham

Fire Spreads on the West Side 51

rushes down from the roof. When he catches sight of Chief Williams, the alderman shakes his head sadly. His mills are bound to catch now, he tells Williams. "And when my buildings go," he adds, "they'll fire the South Side. Nothing can stop it—nothing!" Only minutes later everything on the block is enveloped in flames.

The people living along Canal Street have emptied their homes, dumping furniture helter-skelter into the roadway for safekeeping. But as the flames speed eastward, the piles of tables, chairs, and bedsteads are quickly consumed. The wind picks up burning mattresses, hurling them against the tinder-dry frame houses, where they set off still more blazes. Flaming shingles and pieces of clapboard explode upward through the dense smoke, like the eruption of a small volcano.

Over in the *Chicago Tribune* building at Madison and Dearborn streets a night police reporter, G. P. English, has just finished a story for tomorrow's paper. After turning it in to the city editor, Samuel Medill, the young man gathers up his coat and starts toward the door. A fiery reflection against the window attracts his attention. Another fire? It can't be—not after last night.

Nevertheless, the reporter calls the reflection to

Medill's attention. The city editor, always alert for a good story, tells English to hail a hansom cab and see what's happening. For the next hour the reporter roams through the West Side, watching the flames, taking note of destroyed buildings and their possible losses. When the fire begins springing up all around him, English decides to retreat. Upon his return to the office, Medill asks where the fire is. "Everywhere," says English. He is told to write up the story as quickly as possible. There is still time to get it in the morning edition.

Now the West Side residents are beginning to panic. People are pouring out of their little frame dwellings, some clutching hastily chosen treasures and others carrying kitchen utensils. Dazed by the onslaught of flames, many of the refugees head north a few blocks until they can find a bridge across to the South Side. Others wander aimlessly off toward the west, out of range of the fiery monster.

Chief Williams is still trying to mass his forces toward the north. The fire has not yet reached the area of last night's destruction. He has high hopes that it will stop at the sixteen-acre desert where there is nothing more to burn. Certainly it can't leap the river. His greatest enemy in this battle is the wind—a wind that has many moods tonight. If too many masses of flaming material are carried northward, it could mean chaos. But at the moment Williams knows he must concentrate on stopping this West Side fire.

Spectators from all over the city are crowding into the stricken area to watch the progress of the fire. The size of the crowds often impedes the efforts of the firemen. And there are times when sudden changes in wind cause a mass exodus of frightened onlookers. When a throng around the *Gund* steamer becomes troublesome, foreman Swenie orders one of the firemen to turn his hose on the crowd. Those who are bowled over by the force of the stream get up laughing and beg the firemen to "water down" the rest of the crowd. Last night's fire was great sport, they say, but tonight is even more exciting.

Thomas Ockerby, night superintendent of the Gas Works, is not the only foresighted man in the South Side tonight. Franklin Parmalee has rounded up a number of his employes to assist in wetting down his new stable at Jackson and Franklin streets on the southwestern edge of the business district.

Parmalee, once a clerk on a lake steamer, several years ago acquired a few coaches for transportation along Wabash Avenue. So successful was this venture that he soon formed another company, which provided baggage vans to pick up luggage at the train stations and deliver it to the hotels. It was not long before Franklin Parmalee found himself a wealthy man. Conscious of his newly acquired prominence, he insisted that portraits of his family should be painted on the panels of his coaches. The luxuriant curls of his youngest daughter cover half the side of his favorite coach.

The $80,000 stable of the Parmalee Omnibus and Stage Company has just been completed. The lofts are filled with fresh hay, the stalls are shining, and the horses will be moved in tomorrow. Everything is in readiness for Tuesday's grand opening. Parmalee

Fire Spreads on the West Side

doesn't really feel there is any danger tonight, but he's taking no chances. Pouring a stream of water on the roof and walls is a good precautionary measure.

Roving through the West Side, Benjamin Bullwinkle, captain of the newly formed Insurance Patrol, has been directing his men to put out small awning and roof fires with their portable chemical extinguishers. Ex-alderman Hildreth has been searching for powder to use in blowing up buildings in the line of fire, but he is having no success. He spots Bullwinkle and explains his mission. After some persuasion the Insurance Patrol captain agrees to take Hildreth over to the South Side. Together the men head north in the patrol wagon toward the Lake Street bridge.

Now the great sheets of flame are moving relentlessly with the wind. The fire, which started in Kate O'Leary's barn less than three hours ago, has traveled seven blocks northeast. The area is filled with readily combustible materials. Stores, manufacturing plants, churches, barns, mills, houses, lumberyards, and all the wooden sidewalks over twenty blocks are being attacked with fury. The firemen and their equipment are driven from corner to corner by gigantic waves of fire. Often they escape only seconds before the last exit is cut off.

About eleven o'clock Mayor Roswell B. Mason begins hearing rumors concerning the increasing intensity of the fire out on the West Side. A former Illinois Central Railway official, the mayor is a stocky little man of sixty-six, determined to do his best for Chicago in spite of the fact that his term will be ended next month.

Reports indicate that the fire is more serious than the one last night . . . that all the equipment the city owns is at the scene. Even Chief Williams isn't sure now that the flames can be brought under control. Mason hurries down to the courthouse and sets up a temporary headquarters in the basement office of the police commissioners. By staying here instead of in his third-floor office, he can keep better track of what's going on. Near midnight the mayor sends out urgent telegrams appealing for help as far away as New York City. To Milwaukee's mayor, Harrison Ludington, Mason wires, "Chicago is in flames. Send your whole department to help us." Messages are also dispatched to St. Louis and Cincinnati, asking that fire engines be loaded on railroad cars and rushed to Chicago.

At about this same time Sergeant Kaufman, who administers the United States Weather Signal Office on LaSalle Street, is sending in his nightly report to

Washington. He needs to know the wind speed and goes up to the roof for a look at the anemometer. He has heard the gusts whipping around the building all evening, but the figure on the gauge is startling—sixty miles an hour. Whether this is accurate no one knows. But it is duly recorded on the sergeant's report.

Over at the West Side fire Chief Williams, too, is aware of the increasing force of the wind. Through thick clouds of smoke he can see flying brands being carried swiftly through the air. The whole fiery mass seems to be winging upward in endless waves. But the chief gives no outward evidence of his worries. Instead, he moves quickly from block to block, directing the efforts of the men, giving them much-needed encouragement.

The dense smoke and intense heat are beginning to take their toll among the firemen. Their eyes are burning from the sting of cinders. Beards are scorched, uniforms have been set afire by the falling sparks and hastily beaten out. But these are men of courage, who do not give up in the face of great personal danger.

The equipment is battered, and several of the steamers are badly in need of overhaul. There has also been a serious loss of hoses. Rolling them up and stretching them out again as they were moved from one location to another has caused many breaks. Hundreds of feet of hose have been burned up or trampled upon until water refuses to flow through.

Foreman Alex McMonagle is desperately searching for more hose to replace what the *Long John* has lost. He finds a lengthy piece, hoists it to his shoulder, and starts running toward the steamer. He sees Chief Williams just ahead, and at the same moment his eye catches a terrifying sight.

"Chief, Chief," he screams, "the fire is on the South Side!"

6

Peril for the South Side

Chief Williams' worst fears have been confirmed. The fire has spread to the South Side and his first thought is to get there as quickly as possible. He jumps on the *Washington* hose cart and heads for the nearest bridge. How many people, he wonders, have already been trapped in the burning buildings on the West Side? If the fire should spread, there will undoubtedly be a tragic loss of life as well as property.

Speeding along toward this new outbreak, the chief mentally reviews the topography of the area in which fresh flames are leaping up. Essentially rectangular in shape, the South Side is bounded on the east by the lake, on the north by the Chicago River, and on the west by the winding river branch.

Within the past few years Michigan Avenue, which fronts on the lake, has become a fashionable street for the wealthy. Terrace Row, just north of Congress Street, is considered the height of elegance. This block-long stone building, four stories high, has been divided into eleven separate residences.

Behind Michigan Avenue is the heart of the business district, covering a mile-square area. Wabash Avenue, once almost all residential, is now filled with warehouses and wholesale stores. Along State Street are many of the city's finest retail establishments— Booksellers' Row, Field & Leiter's, and Carson, Pirie, Scott & Company, as well as the eight-story Palmer House, Potter Palmer's famous hotel.

Most of the new office buildings along Dearborn Street were erected during the Civil War boom and the following seven years. The architecture is a hodgepodge of classic, medieval, and Renaissance styles, but the buildings with their marble facades and wrought-iron gingerbread are, nonetheless, very impressive. Chief Williams is thankful tonight that many of the structures are said to be completely fireproof, though

Peril for the South Side

he hopes the conflagration will be stopped long before it reaches Dearborn Street.

In the center of the business district is the showplace of the city—the million-dollar courthouse. Situated in the center of a square block and surrounded by shade trees, a well-maintained lawn, and an iron picket fence, the Athens marble structure is symbolic of Chicago's prosperity. The main part of the building was erected in 1853, but city and county officials complained that the space was inadequate. Flanking wings were added five years later. The basement of the east wing is the county jail, and it is usually well filled.

Atop the central portion of the courthouse is a two-story tower with a cupola where just last spring a four-faced clock was installed—a real help, say Chicagoans, in getting places on time.

In addition, the cupola houses the fire watchman's platform and the five-and-a-half ton bell. The bell has become almost an institution in the lives of the town's inhabitants, pealing out the hours day and night. It has also been rung for the victories at Vicksburg, Gettysburg, and then finally—joyous notes for the fall of Richmond. Its solemn monotones expressed the anguish of the citizens when President Lincoln's body was borne through the streets of the city. Most important of all, though, the clang of the bell is helpful in locating fires.

Despite the apparent affluence of the business district, there is one small section in this area that most people would prefer to ignore. The narrow strip running from Wells Street west to the river fork is known as Conley's Patch—a jungle of cheap boardinghouses, dance halls, and saloons. The little wooden buildings are mere shanties, huddled together along the narrow streets and alleys. Everyone admits the slum is a disgrace. There has been much talk among city officials, but nothing has been done to improve it.

Having reached the site of this fresh outbreak on the South Side, Chief Williams discovers that it is the new stables for the Parmalee Omnibus and Stage Company. The gusty wind had snatched a flaming torch from the West Side and carried it soaring over the river and across two blocks before it dropped on the roof of the stables. Employes of the company, stationed here earlier to stamp out occasional sparks, had done their best but this new blaze caught too rapidly. Now the building is being devoured, and a roofing plant next door is swept up by the flames.

Nearby is the South Side Gas Works, and within minutes another brand sets this building afire. The flames spread so quickly that the firemen are helpless to save anything. However, Chief Williams is relieved to learn that the gas stored in the tanks has already been transferred to the North Side, thanks to the foresight of Thomas Ockerby. There will be no explosion. And Ockerby assures the chief there is probably enough gas left in the pipes to light the South Side for another hour or so.

Fortunately, the West Side fire has begun to subside, now that it has reached the site of last night's conflagration. Chief Williams feels it is safe to move much of the equipment across the bridges to combat the fresh onslaught. In total there are now only fourteen fire engines; the *Gund* was lost less than an hour ago when a building collapsed on top of it. The chief sends orders that two steamers are to stay behind on the West Side, ready to fight anything more that might develop. But twelve engines should be of some help in the new fire.

At 12:20 A.M. the vicious wind snatches another brand and hurls it three blocks to the roof of a tenement in Conley's Patch. Instantly, the tinderbox is a mass of flames. The fire spreads out in all directions, gobbling up the ramshackle buildings in a matter of minutes.

Panic seizes the impoverished residents of the Patch. Narrow streets and alleys swarm with men, women, and children frantic to escape. The fire engines at the scene throw streams of water on the blaze, but they seem to have little effect. The fire surges on, driven by the strong southwest wind.

A shabby washerwoman is seen fleeing along the street, shouldering the week's laundry in a wicker basket. With one free hand she clutches a frying pan and some muffin rings. Huge cinders fall on the freshly starched clothes, setting them smoking, but the poor woman is unaware of what is happening until the burning rags fall on her neck. Howling in dismay, she drops her burden and runs off terrified.

Among the inhabitants of Conley's Patch are many who cannot resist looting as they hurry through the streets. They are breaking into stores, snatching furniture from passing wagons, and robbing passersby who appear to be saving something of value. Violence is becoming more noticeable in this part of the South Side.

As the fire races along the east bank of the river, it laps up several wooden bridges in its pathway, cutting off exits for the frantic crowds. Sixty-year-old Andrew Boyer, tender of the Madison Street bridge, is deter-

Peril for the South Side

mined that his span shall not be destroyed. Each time flames threaten the eastern end he calmly swings the bridge out to the center of the river, while his anxious sons wait in a boat below, ready to rescue their father if he is forced to jump. Boyer's heroic efforts pay off. The flames sweep on northward, and one of the few remaining exits to the West Side is untouched.

Ever since midnight, sleep has been troubled for those living on the North Side. There are many who retired early on this Sunday evening. Those who noticed the flames far to the west believed it was only another fire—nothing to worry about. Within the last few minutes the roar of the wind and the acrid smell of smoke has aroused a number of residents; some stare at the spectacle from second-floor windows. It is a terrifying sight, yet no one is personally alarmed. The Chicago River makes the North Side seem very safe.

There are several businessmen, however, who decide to go down to the South Side to make sure their stores and offices are not in danger. Perhaps they will bring home some of the more valuable records. Among those who have recognized the hideous potential of the flames is Edward Isley Tinkham, cashier of the Second National Bank.

Soon after Conley's Patch catches fire, Mr. Tinkham hurries downtown to his bank. After locating a large trunk, the cashier opens the bank vault and withdraws more than $1,000,000 worth of negotiable securities and $600,000 in currency. Dragging the trunk outside Tinkham sees a policeman and asks him to act as bodyguard. With the assistance of Perry H. Smith, vice-president of the Northwestern Railroad, the cashier lugs the trunk back to his North Side home for safekeeping.

Over at the Post Office on Dearborn Street Alonzo Hannis, one of the postal clerks, has just arrived. Awakened by the noise of the West Side fire, Hannis thought first of the office. The volume of mail here is exceptionally large; only two cities, New York and Philadelphia, outrank Chicago in the amount of business done. Now Hannis asks permission from night superintendent David Green to begin packing letters and packages into sacks for removal. He is warned that taking out mail without permission will be cause for dismissal.

After the night superintendent goes outside to check on the fire's progress, Hannis takes matters into his own hands. He sends a messenger to order out the mail wagons and begins throwing all letters and packages

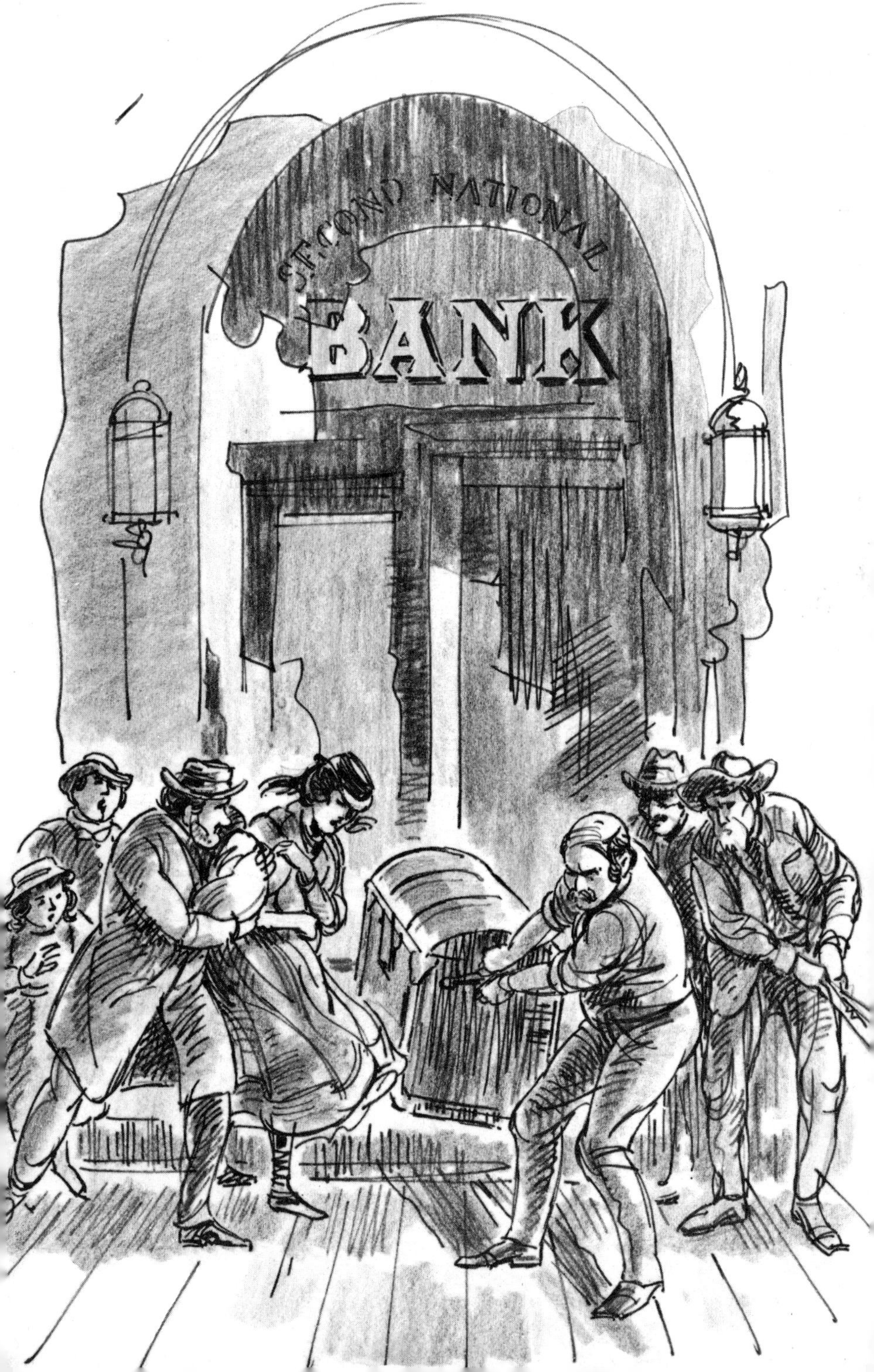
SECOND NATIONAL
BANK

into sacks. Other employes are arriving, and with their help the wagons are soon loaded and started off to the far South Side, out of the path of the flames. Only one small sack is overlooked. It came in four hours late over the Fort Wayne railroad and no one knew it had even arrived.

Meanwhile, James Hildreth has located 2,500 pounds of explosives. He had to break into a powder magazine to get the ammunition, and the watchman on duty at first refused to give him the fuses. But the persuasive Mr. Hildreth explained that only by blowing up buildings in the path of the fire could it be stopped. Finally, the watchman agreed and helped load the explosives into the wagon.

It is close to 1:00 A.M. when Hildreth draws up in front of the courthouse, hoping to find Chief Williams or one of the fire commissioners. Inside the building he has better luck. Mayor Mason is at his desk still writing out urgent telegrams for help. Hildreth says he has a plan to stop the fire. With the mayor's permission he will blow up the Union National Bank on the southwest corner of Washington and LaSalle. This, he is sure, will halt the flames. The mayor, in desperation, agrees to the plan and writes out an order authorizing Hildreth to proceed.

Jubilant over his sudden success, the ex-alderman rushes out of the courthouse and leaps into his wagon. On his way down LaSalle Street he sees Chief Williams and shows him the mayor's order. Williams says he has no firemen available to help Hildreth. But if he is still determined—then be sure everyone is out of the building before lighting the fuse.

Nothing can stop Hildreth now. He enlists several policemen to help carry the kegs of powder into the bank. Placing the explosive material carefully in the basement, he kicks in the heads of the kegs with his boot. After the powder is scattered in rows from one keg to another, Hildreth lights the fuse and runs out of the building. A few minutes later the powder explodes with a tremendous roar, but only the windows are knocked out. The walls are still standing. Hildreth's first attempt to stop the fire has accomplished nothing, but he is not discouraged. The idea is still a good one—he's just had an unlucky break. And he hurries off to hunt up more powder.

Over on State Street Chicago's finest retail establishment is buzzing with activity. It was only four years ago that Marshall Field and Levi Leiter moved their fabulous stock of ladies' finery into the handsome marble-front store erected by Potter Palmer on the corner of Washington and State streets, a store for which they are paying $75,000 annual rent. After the formal opening, a *Tribune* editorialist had commented: "New York cannot boast such a gorgeous palace for the display of dry goods . . . and even Lord & Taylor and A. T. Stewart must hide their diminished heads and acknowledge the supremacy . . . of the Garden City."

When the fire leaped into the South Side both Mr. Field and Mr. Leiter rushed down to their store. Although the flames are still far away, the owners have decided to take action. "We'll save what we can," says Marshall Field. "If the fire comes, it comes, but we will save all we can before that time."

An employe is dispatched to the store's barns to summon drivers and their wagons. Many of the more stalwart clerks are showing up to help; a bucket brigade quickly forms to remove the most expensive wares. From the top floor bolts of Japanese silks, German velvets, and costly black satins are handed down. Four of the brawniest men are stationed at the front doors to guard against looting, while others lift the heavy bolts into waiting wagons. Next come huge packing boxes filled with Belgian laces and French cretonnes.

Peril for the South Side

The drivers bring down their whips with a crack and the wagons rumble off toward the lake shore. There the precious imports are unloaded by heavy-shouldered guards, and the wagons return for more goods.

While the men are carrying out loads of Irish poplins and wool cashmeres the heat suddenly increases. Burning embers are cracking the windows in the buildings across the street. Marshall Field calls for volunteers to help save the store building. Nine men respond and are sent to the mansard roof, where there are three huge water tanks. They begin drenching the roof with buckets of water and spraying streams on the outside walls. Inside, Mr. Field is directing the efforts to keep the store from overheating. He works alongside his men, soaking heavy blankets and draping them out of the open windows.

The pyramiding flames have now destroyed everything in the first four blocks east of the river and are marching toward the business district. Added to the bedlam in the streets is the harsh peal of the courthouse bell, which heightens the terror of the crowds.

Solid sheets of fire are being sucked into the windows of buildings; within seconds the interiors become infernos. Twisting columns that shoot high in the air are seized by hurricane-force winds and sent leaping onto roofs in the next blocks. Then suddenly the pride of all Chicago—the million-dollar courthouse—is in the direct path of the fire.

7

The Flames Surge Northward

For the past hour a number of courthouse employes have been working valiantly on the roof, beating out the snowstorm of sparks that is constantly falling. Firemen from the steamer *Chicago* have come by. But seeing the volunteers on the top of the building, they feel the courthouse is well protected. They have moved their equipment to structures in more imminent danger.

At 1:30 A.M. a huge piece of burning timber sails through a broken window in the courthouse tower, landing on a pile of wood shavings discarded by workmen last week when they were repairing the clock. Within seconds the tower is deluged by flames and the volunteers on the roof run for their very lives. Finding most of the stairwells filled with dense smoke, the men slide down the banisters, scorching only their coattails. Watchman Schafer's final gesture for the protection of Chicagoans is to set the machinery that will keep the great bell tolling automatically.

Ten minutes later the upper floors are a raging furnace and the fire is spreading quickly into all parts of the building. In the basement jail more than a hundred prisoners hear the crackle of the flames, the roar of fire engines clattering by. As the cells begin filling with smoke, there is pandemonium. The prisoners scream and bang on the iron bars, crying to be let out before they are burned alive.

Police Captain Hickey approaches Mayor Mason, still in his basement headquarters, and urges that the prisoners be freed. He and several of his men, Hickey promises, will handcuff those charged with murder and escort them to the North Side where they can be locked up again. Mason agrees and writes out the order before he leaves the burning building.

The cells are opened by the jailer and the prisoners dart out, dazed by their sudden freedom. Just east of the courthouse at the corner of Clark and Randolph is

The Flames Surge Northward

the jewelry store owned by A. H. Miller. Mr. Miller has packed two wagons with his stock, preparatory to leaving the store he knows is doomed. But he has just been told by firemen that the wagons cannot be driven over the hose lying in the street. As the prisoners pass the jewelry store in their flight to safety, the proprietor invites them to take whatever they want from the wagons. Many help themselves.

The courthouse is now wrapped in flames. At 2:12 A.M. the hands slide off one of the clock faces. Three minutes later the great bell plunges to the basement. The roof and walls of the building collapse with a roar that resounds throughout the city.

Brands shooting upward from the crumbling walls of the courthouse are seized by the winds and hurled helter-skelter through the air. One fiery torch is carried across the street to the top of the Merchants' Insurance building, setting fire to the roof. Here the Western Union Telegraph Company has its headquarters. As smoke fills the upper floors, telegraph operators come flying down the stairway. An Associated Press reporter, sending an account of the fire to New York, stops in mid-sentence. The final message to go out over the wires on this early Monday morning reads, THE BLOCK IMMEDIATELY ACROSS THE STREET FROM THE TELEGRAPH OFFICE, ONE OF THE FINEST . . . .

Directly north of the courthouse is the elegant six-story Sherman House, opened just ten years ago. A broad flight of steps leads up to the main entrance on Clark Street, an entrance roofed over by a two-story glass portico. One of the big attractions at the Sherman House is the second-story balcony around the hotel, where visitors enjoy promenading above the noise and dust of the crowded streets. On the flat roof is a railed observation tower that provides a sweeping view of the city.

For the past few hours hotel employes have been busy putting out the flying sparks that are constantly landing on the roof, but most of the hotel's three hundred guests have felt no alarm. As the courthouse collapses the flames leap over the Sherman House and head toward Lake Street. The management heaves a sigh of relief. The hotel has escaped. But an unpredictable wind suddenly turns the fire backward. Smoke begins pouring from the windows at the rear of the building, and before long, tongues of angry flame dart out of the upper floors.

John R. Chapin, an artist for *Harper's Weekly*, arrived from New York yesterday afternoon and registered at the Sherman House. He heard a fire alarm when he turned in about 10:30 last night but he has been sleeping soundly during these early morning hours. Suddenly he is aroused by a loud commotion in the hallway. Night clerk John Hickie is warning the guests to flee. Chapin dresses quickly and manages to escape without incident. He makes his way north to the Randolph Street bridge, takes out his drawing materials, and begins sketching the sights around him. Below his sketch Chapin writes that the fire is "devouring the most stately and massive buildings as though they had been the cardboard playthings of a child."

In the *Chicago Tribune* building on the corner of Madison and Dearborn streets the gaslights have been burning since early last night. Samuel Medill, the city editor, knows that the fire now sweeping through his town is one of the greatest stories of the century. He does not intend to let anyone scoop the *Tribune*.

The *Chicago Tribune,* founded in 1847, is the most influential paper in town, having merged with Deacon Bross's *Democratic Press* in 1855. During the Civil War everyone was avid for news, and the *Tribune*'s circulation more than doubled. Forty-eight-year-old Joseph Medill is the publisher, a man distinguished as much for his staunch Republicanism as for his firm, straight mouth and jutting chin. Co-publisher Deacon Bross was, for a time, more interested in politics than the newspaper world. But having finished a term as lieutenant-governor of Illinois, he is now back in Chicago and has resumed active partnership with Medill.

Although there are four other newspapers in the city, the *Tribune*'s prosperity is obvious. Just two years ago the plant was moved into a new four-story stone structure, headlined at that time as "one of the most complete and elegant news establishments in the world." Its brick division walls and corrugated iron ceilings are considered to be so fireproof that the co-owners have never bothered to take out insurance on the building or its contents.

When Joseph Medill walked into the office about an hour ago, he found that his brother Sam had everything well organized. Reporters in the fourth-floor city room are turning out page after page of copy, sending it down to the basement to be set in type by the compositors.

Medill also learns that his commercial editor, Elias Colbert, has been unusually foresighted. Colbert, after hearing that the Gas Works was destroyed, hurried over to a little wholesale store on Water Street and purchased a box of candles from the night watchman. If the gaslights should go out now, the business of publishing a paper need not be interrupted.

Shortly after the courthouse burns, Deacon Bross makes his appearance at the *Tribune* office. He finds the paper humming, despite the fact that many of the windows are cracking from the heat. Sam Medill says that he has already sent G. P. English, Lewis Meacham, and Elias Colbert up to the roof to make eyewitness reports on those buildings that are burning.

The writers on top of the *Tribune* building are almost blinded by the glare, yet the sight is a spectacular one. From a red-and-black sea of fire, tall spires and pyramids of flame are shooting upward and covering the sky with a myriad of colors. The roar of fire and wind is punctuated by the sounds of falling walls and intermittent explosions. In the streets below, mobs of people are screaming with terror, fighting desperately to find their way to safety. The reporters agree there are enough stories here to fill far more than the morning edition of the *Tribune*.

Meanwhile, Chief Williams has been centering his main line of resistance around the courthouse block, trying every means possible to halt the torrent of fire sweeping in from the southwest. Because dense clouds of smoke have filled the air, the chief has no way of knowing that great columns of flames are jumping blocks ahead of him.

At 2:30 A.M., less than half an hour after the courthouse has collapsed, a shower of sparks leaps northward across the Chicago River, settling upon a train of kerosene-filled cars on the tracks of the Chicago and Northwestern Railroad. The cars ignite with a brilliant flash. The flames begin their march into the North Side—something the residents were certain could never happen.

Within a few moments brands from the railroad cars have set fire to Wright's Stables, a three-story brick building that covers half a block. Several hours ago the owners realized there might be danger. They

The Flames Surge Northward

took the precaution of harnessing their finest horses, ready to leave the building if the situation demanded it. Now the fire strikes so quickly, there is no time to lead the animals to safety.

Although there is a narrow belt of industrial plants and factories just north of the Chicago River, the North Side is primarily a residential area. Here are the luxurious homes of many of the wealthy "first families," some of which occupy an entire block. These impressive structures are often surrounded by beautiful gardens, greenhouses, and a variety of wide-spreading trees.

What was once the "old Chicago—substantial and elegant" has become more varied in recent years. Modest frame dwellings of German and Irish immigrants are intermingled with the finer homes until now nearly 75,000 of the city's population live on the North Side.

Few of the tree-lined streets are paved, and wooden sidewalks are very much in evidence. Every home has a yard, sometimes with a board fence around it. But here there is a more spacious atmosphere. Houses are not huddled together as they are on the West and South sides.

By now almost everyone on the North Side is awake and thoroughly alarmed at the progress of the fire.

Many who watched it with curiosity an hour ago are suddenly aware of the danger to themselves and their homes. They have had little warning. Since the fire has leaped the Chicago River, fresh outbreaks are advancing northeast with frightening intensity. People hastily pack their most precious belongings, load them into carts, wagons, carriages—anything with wheels—and flee north to escape the flames.

One of the first residents on the North Side to lose his home is Dwight L. Moody, the famous evangelist. Sparks from the nearby Wright's Stables have landed on his roof. Seeing their home threatened, Mrs. Moody pleads with her husband to rescue the fine portrait of himself, painted by a prominent artist, G. P. Healey. Reverend Moody tells his wife that he would feel very foolish explaining to inquiring friends that the one thing he has saved is his own portrait. As flames eat their way through the second story, the Moodys leave the house empty-handed.

An hour ago Edward Isley Tinkham arrived on the North Side with the trunk containing the money he rescued from the Second National Bank vault. He was convinced his home was perfectly safe. But now, with the fire racing northward, he too must think of rapid escape.

While his wife gathers the children together, Tinkham dashes outside, frantically trying to flag down one of the wagons racing by on Pine Street. His attempts are futile. So he hurries to a nearby stable and offers the owner $1,000 to haul the precious trunk to safety. The owner refuses, saying that he must think of his own family first. However, there is a buggy with a driver that he can let Tinkham have. The offer is gratefully accepted. Both the trunk and the family are safely stowed in the vehicle, and the driver heads for the lake shore.

Over at 288 Ohio Street the Reverend David Swing, pastor of the Fourth Presbyterian Church, has just returned from an inspection trip through the South Side. On his way home he has seen people everywhere "attempting to put the house into a trunk." Already the streets are clogged with pedestrians and wagons; the only thought in everyone's mind is to get away from the fire. And the Reverend Swing knows he must take his family to safety without delay.

Mrs. Swing has the trunks all packed, but there is no means of conveyance so everything is left behind. The little girls grab up the pet cat and a caged canary, and the family starts northward ahead of the fire, Mrs. Swing clutching her small marble clock. The going is difficult—what with gusty winds blowing smoke and cinders all around them, wooden sidewalks catching fire, and the neat white fences being consumed in a matter of minutes.

The family notices that many of the more luxurious homes are already deserted. Doors are wide open, revealing the fine furnishings, paintings, and silverware that have been abandoned. Wryly, Reverend Swing remarks to his wife that there are "not enough thieves in the North Division to meet the demands of the night."

8

Red Tornado

Meanwhile, back on the South Side, the fire continues to rage through the business district. Its latest victim is the Grand Pacific Hotel, Chicago's newest and most magnificent, which has been designed as the ultimate in luxury and has not yet opened.

The glass-domed carriage court is spacious enough to allow a dozen vehicles to discharge guests at one time. There are exclusive shops in the first-floor rotunda. A wide marble staircase sweeps up to the upper floors, where more than five hundred private rooms are almost ready for occupancy. Extravagant claims have been made in the hotel's advertisements about the new steam-driven "vertical railways" designed to carry Grand Pacific guests upward "as lightly and as smoothly as a cloud rises in the summer air." Now the Grand Pacific is a roaring, crackling mass of flames, its olive-tinted sandstone walls falling with a dull thud.

Several blocks north, at the corner of Dearborn and Lake streets, the Tremont House is also ablaze. For the owner, John B. Drake, it is a heartbreaking sight. There will be no Thanksgiving Day game dinner this year. And Mr. Drake's feast has become an institution for Chicago's elite society. Women are excluded; but when a young man receives an invitation to this annual affair, this means he has been "accepted" by the business community.

There are other memories, too, for the owner. Abraham Lincoln and Stephen A. Douglas used the Tremont's iron-railed balcony as a platform when they spoke here in 1858. And during lecture tours through the west, Ralph Waldo Emerson made the Tremont House his headquarters.

When the fire came, Mr. Drake managed to warn all his guests, but the confusion in the hallways was terrifying. The elevators were no longer working and women were crying hysterically. Nevertheless, everyone escaped, though some were wearing only nightclothes. Drake has managed to save some money from the safe and a pillowcase filled with silver. Everything else is fiery debris.

For several hours the lights in the business district have been growing dimmer and dimmer. By about 2:30 A.M. whatever gas was left in the pipes is gone. The flames provide the only light now. The Washington Street tunnel at this moment is filled with people rushing wildly in both directions. Many are carrying what few valuables they have been able to save, pushing and shoving in order to get through the passageway.

When the gaslights go out, the tunnel is plunged into darkness. One quick-thinking man with a booming voice saves the crowd from panic. He begins shouting, "Keep to the right! Keep to the right!" The cry is taken up by the people and they move forward with almost military precision. Instead of many being crushed to death, they are all able to get through the tunnel without a single accident.

As the fire marches through the business district, the streets are packed with refugees. Those who have come into the South Side out of curiosity, those who have invaded the area to steal whatever they can find, are now caught up in the mob trying to escape the oncoming flames.

The crowds grow thicker by the minute. People are jostling, pushing, shoving, as they surge from one street to another—shouting, cursing, screaming. Confusion is greatest at the intersections and at the approaches to the few remaining bridges, where pedestrians and vehicles tangle in helpless disorder. As avenues of escape, the bridges cannot be counted upon completely. Several bridges, jammed with fleeing victims, break under the unaccustomed weight, sending the refugees flying into the Chicago River.

Added to the terror of the people is the predicament of the trapped animals. Teams of horses, maddened by the terrible roar and the incessant fall of cinders, rush through the streets completely out of control. Some break loose, only to sink to the ground, overcome by fright. Others paw the air, sending out wildly despairing cries.

Dogs lunge through the crowds, enraged by fear.

Underfoot, huge rats scamper out from their hiding places beneath the wooden sidewalks and are crushed by the passing wagon wheels. Overhead, flocks of pigeons rise gracefully into the air, circling far above the shooting flames, their wings reflecting a fiery glow.

Fire billows through the streets, submerging everything in its path. The danger, the frantic excitement, combined with the turbulent winds, bring varied reactions among the refugees. Some men, frenzied by the thought of losing the work of a lifetime, rush about as if they were insane. Others simply accept the situation philosophically, calmly shrugging their shoulders and walking away. A few self-righteous gentlemen wander through the crowds raising their hands and shouting that the fire is the wrath of the Almighty brought down upon Chicago for its wickedness.

In addition to the hordes of people, the streets are jammed with carts, wagons, drays, wheelbarrows— anything that can be used to haul possessions to a safe place. Owners of express wagons are asking and, for the most part, receiving outrageous prices for their services. Some drivers refuse to accept any loads, preferring to rove the streets and pick up whatever they can find for themselves.

Thousands of dollars' worth of books rescued from one of the publishing houses on Booksellers' Row fall prey to the flames. The clerks who carried the volumes outside do not have the $100 fee demanded by the drayman for taking the books to safety.

One ingenious young man decides he will escape at a reasonable price. He bargains with an undertaker to haul a casket over to the West Side for $15. When the driver's back is turned, the young man hops inside. Once the casket is deposited at its destination, the occupant rises up to pay the undertaker. Overcome with fright by this sudden apparition, the poor man drives off without stopping to collect his fee.

Not all wagon owners, however, are trying to make money from other people's tragedies. Young's Horsecar Line on Wabash Avenue is carrying refugees and their possessions without charge. The owner of a bird store has refused offers of $25 for his conveyance; he is hauling furniture for nothing. The Brinks Express Company is lending out wagons as long as its supply lasts.

From the Chicago River southward for almost a mile stretches a grassy area between Michigan Avenue and the lake. It is now piled high with all kinds of furniture, bedding, musical instruments, oil paintings —anything people have been able to rescue. At one end stand the robust guards, protecting the fine imports brought over from Field & Leiter's store.

Several hundred feet offshore the tracks of the Illinois Central Railroad are elevated on a trestle that runs through the water. For the past hour locomotives have been chugging by, hauling long strings of freight cars out of the path of the fire. The shriek of the train whistles adds a sharp note to the nightmare sounds of this early Monday morning.

Shortly before 3:00 A.M. the *Chicago Times* building on the west side of Dearborn Street is a scene of frantic activity. An editorial has been composed and set in type, urging help from nearby cities. The final bulletin reads, "The Very Latest—the entire business portion of the city is burning up and the *Times* building is doomed." But before the paper can go to press the fire leaps over Madison Street and roars through the *Times* establishment like a blowtorch. Fleeing employes manage to save only a few of the files.

When the fire broke out several hours ago, there were nearly two hundred vessels tied up along the banks of the Chicago River. Because most of them are sailing ships, they have to depend on the tugs to move them into Lake Michigan. As the flames spread along the river banks, a number of the ships are in serious danger. Sails, showered with flying sparks, set the vessels ablaze.

Many, however, are saved by the tugs, as well as by the help of cooperative bridge tenders. The tenders swing the spans into the center of the river, thus making a narrow pathway for the ships to glide through to the lake. On shore thousands of frightened refugees clamor for the bridges to be returned to their original positions. Exits to safety are fast disappearing.

One vessel, newly arrived from Buffalo, cannot locate a tug to pull it into the lake. First mate Charles Noble orders that the sails be tightly rolled; all hands aboard are put to work. Half the crew is told to keep the sailcloth soaked down with water, while the remaining members take poles and beat out sparks wherever they fall. Several of the men have their clothes scorched but only minor damage is done to their vessel. Once the fire has passed, all crew members volunteer for patrol duty on shore.

Over in the *Chicago Tribune* office Joseph Medill becomes alarmed for the safety of his fireproof building. Buffeted by gusty winds, the flames are sweeping north and east with increasing rapidity. Medill asks for volunteers from his editorial staff to go with him to the roof. The cement covering on top of the building has been guaranteed to withstand temperatures up to 300 degrees, but with the intensity of heat now in the atmosphere, he wonders how long the roof can last. After collecting buckets and shovels, the publisher leads his men to this point of greatest danger.

Fortunately, there is still plenty of water in the huge tanks that have been erected on the rooftop as a safety precaution. The volunteers drench the falling sparks and beat out small masses of burning fragments that are constantly landing here. So stifling is the air, "like that of a furnace," that the men are forced to run behind the chimney stacks every few minutes "to get a little air and recover from the smoke."

In the offices below, Medill has his reporters working in every room with pails of water and wet cloths. Now that the gas is gone, Elias Colbert's candles have been put to good use. The melting varnish on chairs and desks is doused with water to prevent the furniture from bursting into flame. One foresighted reporter has just put a box of matches into the *Tribune*'s vault. He fears the growing heat might otherwise cause the matches to flare up and set the building on fire.

Down in the basement the pressroom crew is racing against time. Type forms for the inside pages have been delivered from the composing room and are being run off by candlelight. Medill's partner, Deacon Bross, orders the presses to roll on the outside pages as soon as the city room sends down a paragraph bringing the devastation of the fire up to date to this hour. The iron shutters along the south and east sides of the building are fastened securely. Surely there is nothing that can stop the morning edition of the *Chicago Tribune* from reaching its public.

9

North Side Holocaust

The first thrust of fire into the North Side has, fortunately, bypassed the Chicago Historical Society on the corner of Dearborn and Ontario streets. Nevertheless, William Corkran, the librarian and secretary of the society, arrived a short time ago to make certain that all was well. At this moment Corkran is standing in the basement doorway, taking bundles and packages from nearby residents to stack inside for safekeeping. Everyone in town knows that the Chicago Historical Society is completely fireproof. And people are flocking here to deposit their valuables.

When Colonel Samuel Stone, the seventy-two-year-old assistant librarian, hustles into the building, he suggests to Corkran that the basement door should be closed and no more bundles accepted, since houses directly across the street are blazing and the wooden sidewalks have begun to smoke.

While Corkran goes outside to smother the smoldering sidewalks with dirt, Colonel Stone runs upstairs and tries, without success, to break the frame enclosing the priceless Emancipation Proclamation. The front casement is now ablaze, the fire "hanging like feathers on every inch of the window." The colonel decides it is time to leave and flings open the front door, running outside into "one mass of blaze and firebrands flying furiously."

Librarian Corkran, meanwhile, has returned to the building. He knows now that the much-vaunted fireproof qualities of the Historical Society are only a myth. He must save whatever valuables he can. With the janitor's assistance, Corkran unlocks the Emancipation Proclamation from its wall case and wraps it in some battle flags, torn from nearby standards. Just at this moment explosions rock the building and someone shouts that the lecture room is on fire. The frightened librarian drops his precious bundle and leaps down the stairway just as the west side of the building becomes "one great sheet of blaze."

North Side Holocaust

Ever since the fire jumped across the Chicago River, the new water-works pumping station and its high-rising tower have been in the direct path of the showering sparks and brands that are sweeping northeast. Both structures are built of cream-colored stone and are believed to be fireproof. The pumping station's shingle roof has just been replaced with slate, although no one bothered to rip off the Georgia pine shingles before putting on the fireproof material. Merely as a precaution in these early morning hours several employes have been stationed on the roof with buckets of water to douse any sparks that might land there.

At 3:20 A.M. a flaming piece of wood, twelve feet long, sails through the air, barely missing the water tower but striking the northeast window of the pumping station's engine room. Caught and held by one of the ornamental turrets, the blazing torch sets fire to the roof. Before the flames can be put out, the fire eats its way through the shingle under-roof and turns the interior of the pumping station into a thundering inferno. The machinery is twisted into grotesque shapes, the pipes dissolve into molten lumps of lead. Oddly enough, the now-useless water tower across the street still stands, tall and straight.

When Chief Williams is told that the water-works pumping station is gone, he jumps on the nearest hose wagon and rushes up to the North Side to confirm the fearful news. With the water pumps destroyed, Lake Michigan can no longer be used as a reservoir. Only what is left in the mains will be available at the fireplugs.

The firemen all over the city will soon discover that their dwindling supply is gone. Drawing water directly from the lake will be the only way to continue the fight. Shaking his head sadly, Chief Williams knows now that there is probably no way to save the city.

The great columns of fire now roaring through the North Side are very unpredictable. The McCagg mansion on Clark Street is considered one of the finest homes in the city. Here, in a spacious skylighted library, is housed the owner's $40,000 collection of fine books, as well as many valuable paintings. For years the McCagg greenhouses have been a showplace for rare plants. When the capricious flames destroy the mansion, one of the greenhouses is left untouched; the plants inside still bloom.

Not far away on Washington Square is the large three-story frame house of Mahlon B. Ogden, one of Chicago's prominent leaders. Beautifully landscaped and surrounded by tall elm trees, the property covers an entire block. In these early morning hours Ogden's home is filled with friends and strangers alike—peo-

North Side Holocaust

ple who have come here hoping the fire will not attack this open space.

When sparks begin falling on the mansard roof, Mr. Ogden and several of his friends arm themselves with buckets and brooms. Climbing up to the top of the house, they begin beating out the small fires wherever they start. Others soak carpets and blankets in water and hang them on the sides of the house over the windows. Just as the flames seem about to engulf the mansion, the wind suddenly shifts. Mahlon B. Ogden's home is left standing, the only residence for many blocks around.

People suddenly driven from their homes by the fire are reacting in odd ways. The things they choose to save are often absurd. One man rushes about wildly searching for important business papers, only to discover after he is out in the street that he is carting away an empty cigar box. From his desk a teacher snatches what he believes is a paid-up life insurance policy. Too late he finds that he has grabbed up last year's receipted bills. One well-dressed man hurries along the street with a rubber tube and the broken standard of a drop-light. Another trundles a cook stove shoved into a wheelbarrow, while on his back is strapped a featherbed.

A number of homeowners are burying property in

their own yards before trying to escape. Silverware and pianos seem to be the most popular items to save, although digging a hole large enough to hold a piano takes more time than many can spare. One cautious homeowner wants to be sure his fuel supply will be safe. Spading up a large area, he carefully deposits all the coal from his basement before he leaves.

The streets and sidewalks are now filled with pedestrians and conveyances of every description. Bedding, trunks, bundles of clothing, are sometimes abandoned when the flames come too close and the people must run for their very lives. The horrors of the early-morning flight are intensified by maddened horses that have escaped from burning stables and plunge through the crowds, kicking and trampling anything in their pathway. The only light is the piercing glare from the seething flames; yet it is almost as bright as midday.

For the thousands scurrying northward, two graveyards adjoining Lincoln Park offer sanctuary, at least for a while. Burials ceased some years ago; there are many open pits from which caskets have been removed to cemeteries farther north. These pits serve as temporary refuge from the rain of sparks and cinders. Families huddle together to protect their eyes from the blinding smoke. But when the surrounding trees begin to catch fire, there is a mass exodus. For the most part, the people trudge along quietly, too frightened to talk, not knowing where they are going but simply impelled forward by the wall of fire behind them.

Residents whose escape north or westward has been cut off by the fire now run to the lake shore just north of the Chicago River, an area long known as the Sands. Here thousands gather—families of great wealth and immense poverty, all drawn together by a common fear.

Many of the women are still in nightgowns, with wrappers drawn tightly around them. Most of the men have had time to pull on only trousers, with their nightshirts hastily tucked inside. But there are a few people who have taken time to dress, with the thought of saving at least part of their wardrobes. One wealthy matron is wearing two silk dresses from Paris. Over her costume she has flung a raincoat, the pockets of which are filled with opera glasses and silver spoons. An elderly grandmother, upon reaching the beach, finds it is impossible to sit down on the sand. The six dresses she is wearing one on top of another are too great an impediment. Nevertheless, she knows she will have clothing after the fire has burned itself out.

Most people have brought a few valuables—plates, boxes of important documents, silverware—whatever they prize most. Elegant carpets are serving as temporary shelters, while elaborately carved mirrors reflect the spreading flames. Mattresses dragged to the lake shore are continually catching fire, and there is a steady procession to the water's edge to fill buckets that can be used to douse the bedding.

Amidst all the furor along the beach, the devotion of one couple is very touching. The husband is ill and his wife has somehow managed to bring him to the water's edge. Having secured an old piano packing case, she has placed the box on its side, with the bottom facing in the direction of the flames. There she has made a bed for her ailing husband. A piece of candle is fastened to a wire hung from the top. Now the ingenious woman sits calmly beside him, reading aloud.

When the fire threatens to encircle the Sands, many people drive into the water as far as their horses can safely go. Then they clamber up on top of the wagons to wait out the fire storm. Others stand in water at various depths, from knees to waists—all with their backs to the flames raging around them.

In this rain of falling embers, some of the men are

burying their wives and children in the sand, leaving only a small hole through which to breathe. The husbands splash these mounds with water and then dash into the lake, standing chin-deep and breathing through wet handkerchiefs to revive themselves. For hours they continue running back and forth, dumping water on the protective sand-graves.

Believing that even the Sands may no longer be safe, several of the refugees try to reach the lighthouse pier that extends out into the lake. Here they can be out of the direct path of the fire. Edward Isley Tink-

North Side Holocaust

ham, the banker, uses this mode of escape for his family, while the driver takes the buggy into the water as far as the horses can go. Turning the $1,600,000 trunk on end, the driver perches on top of his valuable cargo. An hour later he shows up on the pier, dragging the precious trunk behind him.

Another man who seeks shelter for his family on the lighthouse pier is Isaac N. Arnold. The Arnold property has long been one of the showplaces of the North Side—an impressive brick mansion surrounded by broad lawns and beautiful gardens. Mr. Arnold is a lawyer and former congressman whose tastes are literary. His large library, his ten volumes of manuscript letters from McClellan, Grant, Chase, Lincoln, Farragut, and other notables—all have been destroyed in these early morning hours. Arnold had waged a valiant battle to save his home. But without water, the effort was futile. He is thankful that his family is with him, that they can find a small measure of safety on the pier.

Now the columns of flames move through the residential areas of the North Side with the force of a tornado, snatching up burning buildings and throwing them down on top of others. Superheated air is creating a draft that sends fire hurtling along the rooftops with unbelievable force.

Whole blocks are bursting into flames simultaneously, fed by the frame houses, the wooden sidewalks, and the piles of abandoned furniture. Strangely enough, in the midst of all this tragedy, there are a few people who have kept their sense of humor. One man, who has lost both his business and his home, is wandering around with a portion of a carved mantlepiece slung across his shoulders. "That's all there is now," he laughs, "but I'm going to build a house to fit it!"

10

Out of Control

With the water supply now completely gone, Chief Williams is simply fighting a delaying action on the South Side. A number of the fire fighters have quit and gone home. But the chief is determined to do what he can. Bone-weary though he is, Williams continues to direct what is left of his dwindling forces. The property loss is overwhelming, and he shudders to think how many people have been killed.

By 4:00 A.M. more than half of the business district has been consumed by the fire. Less than an hour ago the stone Post Office building caught. Iron shutters for the basement and first-floor windows had been removed four months ago when repairs were made. Due to someone's carelessness, the shutters had never been put back, and it was through these unprotected windows that the fire entered the building. Thanks to the foresight of postal clerk Alonzo Hannis, though, all letters and registered mail have been saved.

Most of the theaters are gone, and all the city's newspaper buildings, with the exception of the *Chicago Tribune*. Farwell Hall, where George Francis Train predicted this calamity in his Saturday night lecture, is burning. Wood's Museum, once the home of "the greatest collection of curiosities in the West," is a smoking mass of rubble.

Yet in the southeastern part of the South Side, there is still hope. This section is out of the direct path of the wind. Nothing on State Street has yet been touched, but with no water available, survival now is simply a matter of luck.

Along Wabash Avenue, one block east of State Street, great crowds of refugees gather, described by a *Tribune* reporter as "looking like a routed army." With them they have brought "valuable oil paintings, books, pet animals, musical instruments, toys, mirrors, bedding—ornamental and useful articles of every kind."

Friends meeting here cannot recognize each other, so blackened are their faces by the smoke and dust. Women are holding children in their arms while the men guard the few possessions they have been able to rescue. One family has saved a coffee pot. Raking together some embers from the street, they are cheerfully boiling coffee. For the most part, however, the people stand in silence, horrified by the deafening noises several blocks away. And everywhere the air is saturated with the stench of burning wood.

More and more refugees are spilling onto the "broad green" that slopes away from Michigan Avenue to the water's edge. Many are dazed by the magnitude of the flames, the terrifying yet awesome beauty of the spectacle they are witnessing. Yet all the while there is the searing heat, the hail of sparks that set clothing afire and must be beaten out instantly. Several blocks toward the west a Catholic church collapses, but the burning cross on the steeple is caught up by the wind and hangs in mid-air—an eerie phenomenon that causes those who see it to bow their heads and cross themselves.

In the White Stockings ball park along the lake front between Randolph and Washington streets several men are trying to bury silverware and other valuables. A lone policeman attempts to stop them, saying they will be fined for "defacing the ball grounds."

Around 5:00 A.M. the fickle wind shifts again, this time sweeping the flames back toward Dearborn Street, heading directly for Mr. Crosby's luxurious Opera House. The colorful posters advertising tonight's opening concert with Theodore Thomas conducting are ignited, and the newly redecorated concert hall is caught up in a whirlpool of fire. Soon afterward, Mr. Thomas and his musicians pull into the Twenty-second Street railroad station, only to be told that the Opera House is nothing but rubble now. The maestro and his company leave immediately for St. Louis.

After the group of businesses contained in the Reynolds block on Dearborn Street are consumed, one man is seen poking about the smoking debris shortly before dawn. A curious bystander asks what in the world he is doing. The answer is simple, says the man. He is merely feeling the bricks to see whether or not they are cool enough yet to start rebuilding.

The sun comes up on this Monday morning at 6:05 A.M.—"a red ball glowing dully through the pall of smoke" that enshrouds the burning city. The temperature is unofficially recorded at 67 degrees, with a wind blowing in from the southwest at twenty-five miles an hour. In Washington, D.C., the United States

Out of Control

Weather Office issues the following prediction: "The probabilities are that the threatening weather in the Missouri Valley will probably move northeastward over Lake Michigan."

In less than an hour after sunup the fire begins its savage march south along State Street. On the roof of the Field & Leiter building volunteers are still stamping out flames. By 7:00 A.M. the Allen-Mackey Carpet Company next door is swathed in fire. Flaming brands pierce the wet carpets Marshall Field and his helpers have so carefully draped over the windows.

Within minutes each floor is enveloped by fire. Volunteers escaping from the roof find the stairways blocked by dense smoke. Fighting their way down, the men emerge with inflamed eyes, singed beards, and scorched clothing—but thankful to be alive. Mr. Field now asks several of his faithful employes to go over to the lake shore and find the merchandise that was taken there hours ago for safekeeping.

Looters are stealing anything they can get their hands on; Marshall Field wants the fine imports moved out to Mr. Leiter's home at Twenty-third Street and Prairie Avenue, away from all danger. Leave the blankets, bedding, and inexpensive coats, the owner directs. They can be given to refugees later. But for now the fine laces, silks, and shawls must be taken where the fire cannot possibly destroy them.

Soon a long procession of Field & Leiter delivery wagons, as well as the owners' buggies, begins creaking its way toward the lake shore. Two and a half million dollars' worth of stock and furnishings still in the building must be abandoned.

Farther south on State Street stands the Mandel Brothers' new store, which is to open its doors for the first time this morning. When Emanuel Mandel arrives at the scene, his building is still untouched. Firemen are playing heavy jets of water on the walls but there is not enough pressure left in the mains to send the streams above the first floor. Mandel offers the firemen five hundred dollars if they will save his building. But the foreman replies that even five million couldn't save it now. Ten minutes later the store that hasn't yet opened is a pile of burning rubble.

Although many of Chief Williams' fire fighters have given up, there are still a number of men trying to perform their duties. Yet with the water supply gone, it is a hopeless battle. Everyone is completely exhausted —with one exception. Ex-alderman Hildreth has spent these early morning hours dashing through the streets, ripping burning awnings from building fronts, and

Out of Control

helping rescue merchandise from stores already afire. His energy seems boundless.

After Hildreth had used up all his explosives, to no avail, he had begged Mayor Mason to send for more powder. The Mayor promised he would, but the new wagonload of powder does not arrive until almost 8:00 A.M. Someone had suggested that it should be stored on the lake front away from the rain of sparks. Refugees assembled along the beach threaten to hang the frightened wagon driver for bringing a load of explosives into their midst. But a police captain intervenes and explains that the powder is for a good purpose—to blow up buildings and devise a fire-break.

Hildreth, notified that the powder has arrived, hurries over to the wagon. Plotting his course carefully, he decides that certain buildings along Wabash Avenue near Washington Street will best serve his purpose. Assisted by Police Sergeant Lewis Lull, he lugs the kegs into the cellars of these buildings and lights the fuses. Shortly afterward loud explosions are heard, testifying to Hildreth's success. But the onrushing flames merely leap over the rubble, and once again the ex-alderman's efforts are in vain.

Farther south at State and Quincy streets is the imposing hotel owned by Potter Palmer, known to everyone in town as the Palmer House. Palmer, a native New Yorker, had come to Chicago in 1852 and opened a dry-goods store on Lake Street. Within ten years his retail establishment was making history with its innovations. The merchant ran large ads in the newspapers, used window displays, and allowed women customers to buy on approval—something no one had ever dreamed of doing.

During the early days of the Civil War Potter Palmer borrowed heavily from the banks and crammed his warehouses with cotton and woolen goods. By the time the conflict ended, he was a millionaire. The retail business no longer interested him, and he sold the store to two enterprising young clerks, Marshall Field and Levi Leiter.

With his profits Palmer invested heavily in real estate, concentrating on State Street. Heretofore it had been only a narrow dirt road lined with cheap houses and sheds. Buying up all the property for nearly a mile, he succeeded in having State Street widened to one hundred feet and paved with Nicholson wood blocks. Along this street he constructed thirty-two buildings—stores, businesses, and a large hotel. Just last spring the millionaire started construction of another hotel, a new and larger Palmer House one block north.

Out of Control

The building is not yet finished, but Palmer expects it to be the largest and best hostelry in the midwest. The new hotel is Palmer's wedding gift to his bride, the former Bertha Honoré. They hope to move into their elegant suite within a few months.

When the fire broke out on the South Side last night, the Palmer House guests were thrown into a state of panic. Hotel employes quickly calmed them by displaying the fire hoses installed on every floor. As the flames appeared to bypass State Street, everyone relaxed. This morning those who hurriedly removed their baggage to the street are bringing it back inside the hotel. A number of guests are enjoying a leisurely breakfast in the dining room. Others are chatting in small groups in the lobby.

Suddenly and without warning the fire sweeps southward. The building next door is burning . . . the alarm is sounded in the hotel . . . and the guests scatter helter-skelter into the street. Minutes later flames coil around the Palmer House like a giant snake. As the walls collapse, the hot bluish flames jump across to the new Academy of Design on Adams Street.

Artists with studios there arrived as early as 1:00 A.M. Hours later, when it appeared that the fire might be a threat, they began carrying out many of the academy's three hundred paintings. Now, with the building wreathed in smoke, the artists are grateful that the mammoth "Battle of Gettysburg" painted by Peter Rothermel has been rescued. It was purchased a week ago by the State of Pennsylvania; now it will be possible to send this work of art to its new owner.

As the fire continues to travel along State Street, it appears that the new Palmer House, still under construction, may be caught up in the conflagration. John Mills Van Osdel, the architect, grabs some drawings of the building and buries them in a pit in the base-

Out of Control

ment, using two feet of clay and wet sand as a covering. Within fifteen minutes the building is attacked and heavily damaged. So intense is the heat of the fire that out in the center of State Street the iron streetcar rails lunge upward in grotesque shapes.

Over on Dearborn Street the *Chicago Tribune* building still stands "like a mailed warrior, lightly scathed by rolling flames." In the composing room John Tippett has just set the final sentence for the morning edition: ". . . and the wind raging, and the fire burning, and London and Paris and Portland outdone, and no Milton and no Dante on earth to put the words together!"

The steady whir and thump of the Hoe cylinder-type presses in the basement is almost drowned out by the terrible roar from the streets. As the last sheet, printed on one side, comes off the press, McVicker's Theatre across the alley bursts into flames. The stouthearted pressmen vow they will get the paper out "even if the roof over their heads should take fire."

About 9:00 A.M. the basement begins filling with smoke. The rollers on the presses are melting from the heat. One of the men runs up the five flights of stairs to the roof to tell Joseph Medill what is happening.

The smoke is so dense, he says, that the men cannot remain any longer. Besides, the water is gone and there is no way of getting up steam to operate the presses. At this moment Medill realizes that all hope of printing his paper must end. The important thing now is to be sure his men escape without accident.

He tells the weary volunteers on the roof to leave at once, then races through the building to alert everyone else. Some of the men, exhausted, are asleep on the scorched floors. They are jerked abruptly to their feet and told that the situation has become desperate. The publisher asks each man to take as many of the bound volumes of the *Tribune,* prior to 1860, as he can carry. Medill does not worry about the later issues; he has a complete set of those at home.

Running past the pressroom, reporter Elias Colbert grabs up a copy of the outside pages already printed. He is the only person in the city who has even half a newspaper to read this morning. The front-page story is headlined, "While the Fire Raged."

Once outside, the fleeing employes find that the bound volumes they are carting away are bursting into flames from the intense heat. The *Tribune*'s files are quickly abandoned as the men run for their lives.

After making sure that everyone is out of the building, Joseph Medill dashes east along Madison Street.

Out of Control

Looking back, he sees the flames from McVicker's Theatre leaping across the alley, catching up one side of the *Tribune* building in a gigantic swoop. There is a small measure of comfort for Medill, though, in knowing that his great establishment has been, by several hours, "the last newspaper to succumb" to the fire.

11

Continuing Calamity

Once the *Chicago Tribune* building begins to burn, Deacon Bross, Medill's partner, knows there is nothing more to be done here. He mounts his horse and rides over to Michigan Avenue. Threading his way through the crowds in a "hopeless frame of mind," he heads south to his home in the elegant Terrace Row. Residents here have already become aware that the supposedly fireproof building is not impervious to danger; they are moving furniture onto the avenue, loading valuables into any conveyance they can locate.

When Bross arrives home, he finds an express

Continuing Calamity

wagon standing empty in front of his residence. Believing that his daughter has hired the wagon to haul away their belongings, Bross begins loading all their finest furniture into it. Only after the driver leaves does he learn that the man is an imposter who has just made off with all their possessions.

Going back up his front steps, the publisher meets a stranger coming out of his house, a man who looks "decidedly corpulent." Bross stops him, saying, "My friend, you have on a considerable invoice of my clothes, with the hunting suit outside." Then, sighing wearily, he adds, "Well, go along. You might as well have them as to let them burn."

By 11:00 A.M. Michigan Avenue is crowded with vehicles of every description. Families are trying to escape from the fire; express wagons are heaped with furniture the owners hope to save. Throngs of men, women, and children rush along the sidewalk, their arms filled with possessions hurriedly chosen. One woman carries an empty bird cage; another holds a battered workbox in one hand and some dirty baskets in the other. Many are so dazed by the onslaught of fire that they have grabbed whatever is handy, without forethought or judgment.

Early this morning, while the flames were still raging well to the west of Michigan Avenue, one foresighted businessman arrived at his office across from the White Stockings' baseball stadium. George M. Pullman had too great an investment to take any chances.

Pullman remembered well that first trip to Chicago in 1857 when he was coming to help elevate the buildings along Lake Street. He had spent a sleepless night on the train from Buffalo; the tiny pigeonhole that passed for a berth was much too narrow for comfort. Then and there Pullman had resolved to do something about it.

Two years later, with profits from the buildings he had raised, the ingenious Pullman began experimenting with old railroad cars. Being a cabinetmaker by trade, he produced a $20,000 model in 1864. Named *The Pioneer,* the walnut-paneled car was luxuriously upholstered and carpeted. There were two staterooms, sections of cushioned seats that could be converted into beds at night, upper berths that let down from above, and two washrooms.

Newspapers reported *The Pioneer* was a marvel, but the railroad companies pronounced it too expensive. For a year and a half the car stood useless; then, unexpectedly, Pullman's fortunes changed. After Pres-

Continuing Calamity

ident Lincoln was assassinated, his body was brought back to Illinois. When the funeral train stopped in Chicago, Mrs. Lincoln collapsed from exhaustion. She asked to be sent on ahead to Springfield, and George Pullman offered his model car for her trip. So glowing were the press reports that it was not long before the public began clamoring for the comfortable new cars. By the time the Pullman Palace Car Company was incorporated three years later, the sleepers had been adopted by all Western railroads as well as by the New York Central.

Early this morning, though the danger to his Michigan Avenue office still seemed remote, Pullman insisted that all the files, desks, chairs, and supplies be loaded on a railroad car and moved out to his new stables at Eighteenth Street and the lake. Now that the fire is beginning to roar southward along Michigan Avenue, the designer of the famous sleeping car knows that his company will probably be one of the few able to resume business almost immediately.

In the exclusive Chicago Club at 168 Michigan Avenue, between Adams and Jackson, several members have gathered for a late-morning breakfast. They are men of prominence, most of whom have lost both their homes and their businesses in the early morning hours. Nevertheless, they have met together to drown their sorrows.

Before breakfast is finished, the clubhouse catches fire and the gentlemen make a hasty exit, but not until they have filled their pockets with cigars and carried out a red satin sofa. Pushing their way through the crowds, they cross Michigan Avenue and place the sofa carefully on the beach. Here the members smoke their cigars in comparative luxury.

Ever since the Tremont House was destroyed very early this morning, its owner, John B. Drake, has been wandering along the streets, doing what he could to help those who needed assistance in rescuing their possessions. He hears much conversation about how Chicago will never recover from this devastating fire . . . the city is finished. But Drake does not believe it. Chicago's resiliency may be put to a severe test, but the men of vision who have built this city will certainly not go down to defeat.

About noon Drake decides to go to his boardinghouse and try to get some sleep. He passes the Michigan Avenue Hotel at Congress Street just south of Terrace Row. It is directly in the path of the onrushing fire—but is still untouched. The *Brown* and the *Rice* steamers are stationed nearby and drawing water

Continuing Calamity

directly from the lake as the firemen splash down the hotel's outer walls.

Drake has a sudden intuition. He strides into the hotel lobby and confronts the distraught proprietor with an offer to buy the hotel's lease and all its furnishings. The owner cannot believe Drake's offer is a serious one. Why, the hotel will be in flames any minute now. But Drake persists, taking out $1,000 from the Tremont's cash box and giving it to the owner as a down payment. Copies of a contract-to-buy, if the hotel survives, are hastily drawn and properly witnessed by several fleeing guests.

With his copy of the contract tucked in his pocket, Drake leaves the Michigan Avenue Hotel, noting that Terrace Row next door has begun to burn. Hurrying on southward, he wonders whether he has just made a very stupid bargain.

The owner of the former Tremont House is not the only person this morning who is confident about Chicago's future. The popular author and editor, John S. Wright, is striding down nearby Wabash Avenue when he meets his publisher, D. H. Horton. Horton's firm has just brought out Wright's *Chicago, Past, Present and Future.* Both men, blackened by soot and smoke, have escaped from burning buildings, but Horton pauses long enough to ask the author what he now thinks of Chicago's future. Without a moment's hesitation, Wright answers, "I will tell you what it is, Horton. Chicago will have more men, more money, more business within five years than she would have had without this fire."

Shortly after noon it finally becomes apparent that the fire in the South Side is beginning to taper off. Chief Williams now hopes that the flames may be stopped at Harrison Street just south of Congress. An hour ago he ordered a number of engines to take up positions along Harrison Street running east to Lake Michigan. By pumping directly from the lake, water can be relayed to the fire with each engine "feeding the next in line." The West Side fire is now almost completely out, and there is no danger that leaping flames may slip in behind the fire fighters.

Over on the lake shore Deacon Bross sits disconsolately beside the few possessions he has saved. As the flames devour Terrace Row, "they wrap up the whole block and away it floats in black clouds over Lake Michigan." However, the luxurious marble-and-stone residence block is the last building to burn on the South Side. Chief Williams' strategy has worked; the fire is contained at Harrison Street. More than seventeen hours have elapsed since Patrick O'Leary's barn began smoking on DeKoven Street. But now—at last —the monster is under control here in this area. The weary chief sighs.

After leaving the *Tribune* building, Joseph Medill went home "more dead than alive." He pulled off his boots and threw himself down on his bed. But sleep was fitful with a "rush of frightful dreams." Two hours later he is having a hasty breakfast when he suddenly remembers a job-printing plant stored in a ramshackle building at No. 15 Canal Street on the West

Side. He hurries out to find the owner and rents the plant on the spot. There is neither a steam power press nor any engine . . . this can come later. The limited type is composed mainly of numerals and capitals, but the headquarters of the *Chicago Tribune* is once again established. Messengers are dispatched all over town to tell the staff to come to work as soon as possible.

The *Evening Journal* has moved into a building next door. With characteristic generosity, Joseph Medill lends the rival paper his limited equipment for a fire edition to be printed this very afternoon. On a single sheet the *Journal* headlines the extra:

THE GREAT CALAMITY OF THE AGE!
Chicago in Ashes!
The South, the North, and a Portion of the
West Divisions of the City in Ruins

All the Hotels, Banks, Public Buildings, Newspaper
Offices and Great Business Blocks Swept Away

The Conflagration Still in Progress

Chicago is burning! Up to this hour of writing (1 P.M.) the best part of the city is already in ashes . . . The entire South Division, from Harrison Street north to the river, almost the entire North Division, from the river to Lincoln Park, and several blocks in the West Division are burned.

Continuing Calamity

So reads the extra—the only newspaper published on this day, Monday, October 9, 1871, in the city of Chicago.

By afternoon many of the more responsible citizens are concerned about law and order for this stricken city. Allan Pinkerton is one who takes drastic action. Pinkerton is a Scotsman who came to the United States and settled in Chicago twenty-nine years ago. Although he was asked to be the city's first police detective, he soon found the job was utterly hopeless.

Pinkerton resigned and formed his own agency, taking as his trademark a huge eye with the words "We Never Sleep" printed underneath. He guarded Abraham Lincoln on his inaugural journey from Springfield, Illinois, to Washington, D.C. Soon after the outbreak of the Civil War he assisted in organizing a federal secret service and was also active in Chicago's underground railway activities for escaping slaves during the war.

The watchful Mr. Pinkerton has just issued orders to his large force of private policemen that they are to be responsible for the ruins in the business section. His warning is stern:

> Any person stealing or seeking to steal any property in my charge, or attempting to break open the safes, as the

men cannot make arrests at the present time, they shall kill the persons by my orders. No mercy shall be shown them, but death shall be their fate.

Mayor Roswell B. Mason is also busy this afternoon, organizing his city to meet the needs of the great catastrophe. His first proclamation reads in part:

> Be it known that the faith and credit of the city of Chicago is hereby pledged for the necessary expenses for the relief of the suffering . . . . With the help of God, order and peace and private property shall be preserved. The City Government and committees of citizens pledge themselves to the community to protect them, and prepare the way for a restoration of public and private welfare. It is believed that the fire has spent its force, and all will soon be well.

Officers and men of the Fire and Health departments are deputized as special policemen. A temporary city hall and relief headquarters is set up in the First Congregational Church at Washington and Ann streets. The mayor asks Melville Stone to take his horse and buggy and tour the West Side, telling refugees to go to the church for food and clothing.

Mr. O. W. Clapp, a member of the Chicago Board of Trade, is appointed to distribute whatever arrives on the South Side by way of supplies. The energetic Mr. Clapp locates a warehouse still standing beside the Chicago River and directs that all railroad relief trains be unloaded here.

There is little doubt that Chicago is already beginning to cope with the problems inflicted by "the terrible calamity."

12

Will It Never End?

Although the fire is under control on the South Side, it is still raging through the North Side. Fifteen hours ago all the handsome buildings that made Chicago "Queen City of the West" were standing proud and strong in the quiet of a Sunday evening. Now, everything has vanished. And the homes of the men who built Chicago are being consumed.

Block after block has been leveled. Trees have become charred silhouettes against the skyline. Houses have disappeared, leaving only a litter of ashes with an occasional gutted brick wall still standing. Here

Will It Never End?

and there an iron stove or parts of twisted plumbing are ironic testimony of the durability of the metal.

Around seven this morning the great McCormick Harvester Works along the north bank of the river was swept up by the flames. Since midnight Cyrus McCormick had been at the scene directing the fire-preventive measures of his faithful employes.

Cyrus Hall McCormick, a native of Rockbridge County, Virginia, had invented his famous reaper long before he moved to Chicago. By the mid-1840's the ambitious young man was convinced that the great future of farming lay in the wheat fields of the western prairies. After an exploratory expedition he determined that Chicago was the site of greatest promise, and in 1847 he came here to establish himself. His factory was soon pointed out with great pride by the town's residents.

The Civil War brought prosperous times to the McCormick Harvester Works. Secretary of War Stanton paid high tribute to the inventor when he said: "The reaper is to the North what slavery is to the South. By taking the places of men on the farms, it releases them to do battle for the Union and at the same time keeps up the nation's supply of bread. Without McCormick's invention I feel the North could not win."

Cyrus McCormick is a meticulous man who never takes chances with fire hazards. Vast quantities of paint, wood, and oil were stored in his factory, but he always had watchmen guarding his property, day and night. Now, despite heroic efforts, the fire has taken its toll. Two thousand new farm machines have been destroyed, along with all the manufacturing equipment.

By noon the fire has demolished as great an area on the North Side as it has on the South and West sides combined. And the flames sweep onward, completely out of control. The air becomes suffocating. Smoke pours from the windows of many homes long before they are caught up by the fire. There is an endless procession of people, carts, wagons, and animals —all fleeing from the onrushing danger.

Out on the lighthouse pier the Arnolds and the Tinkhams watch apprehensively as the flames creep nearer and nearer the shoreline. About 3:00 P.M. the tug *Clifford* comes steaming up to the pier, having just escaped from the Chicago River. The paint is blistered but the hull has not been harmed. Isaac Arnold has an idea. Will the captain take the refugees aboard and try to get through the river to the forks and up the North Branch, where they can land in safety?

Will It Never End?

At first the captain hesitates. The bridges at State, Rush, Clark, and Wells streets have all burned and fallen into the river. The channel, he says, is filled with charred beams as well as the floating wrecks of ships already burned. It will be a very dangerous passage—if they can get through at all.

Banker Tinkham is ready to take the chance; he *must* get his precious trunk of money to safety. He adds his pleas to those of Arnold. Finally the captain agrees, and the refugees clamber onto the deck.

Women and children are directed to stay in the enclosed pilot house, where the windows can be clamped down tightly. The men are to cover themselves with wet sheets and lie flat inside the bulwarks. The captain gets up a good head of steam, attaches the hose to its pumps, and prepares to spray water over the deck as the tug glides through the red-hot area.

Fires are burning on both banks as the little boat thrusts its snub nose into the Chicago River. Cautiously the captain proceeds past Rush Street. But at State Street the debris of the fallen bridge makes the going even more difficult. The captain slows down, fearing that the propeller may become ensnarled in some of the blackened timbers. The water pumps give out. However, the tug cannot stop now . . . it steams on at what the refugees feel is "a snail's pace."

The captain maneuvers the little boat past Wells Street. Slowly, carefully, he turns into the north branch of the river and the passengers shout, "We are through, we are through!" When the tug finally docks, the people are jubilant. They have arrived safely after one of the strangest tugboat runs ever made on the Chicago River. Banker Tinkham and his family immediately take a train to Milwaukee, where the worried cashier can at last deposit the cargo of money in a bank vault.

Meanwhile, ex-alderman Hildreth brings his powder wagon up to the North Side, hoping to blow up more buildings. He tries to enlist assistance from those hurrying through the streets, but has no success. The very word "powder" frightens everyone. Eventually, Hildreth gives up and goes home, saddened by the fact that no one has ever really taken his efforts seriously.

Thousands and thousands of residents on the North Side have abandoned their homes to the fire, but there is one young man who is determined that his dwelling shall not be destroyed. Policeman Richard Bellinger, married just last summer, had presented his bride with her dream house, a small white cottage on Lincoln Place near the park. Very early this morning he began preparing for what he was sure would be an attack.

Meticulously, Bellinger tore up the sidewalk in front of his house and ripped out the picket fence, chopping up all the wood for kindling. Then he raked up all the dead leaves in his yard; with the leaves and the wood he started a small bonfire. Once they were burned, he carefully tamped out all the embers. Then he covered the roof and outside walls of his cottage with wet carpets and blankets, announcing to his neighbors that "live or die", he would not give up his house.

As the fire advances, Bellinger is ready. He has pails of water drawn from his cistern and throws them on the flaming torches that land on his roof. When the water is gone, the policeman runs to the basement and fills the pails with cider. As the blankets begin to burn, they are liberally doused. Hour after hour he fights on, with the flames whirling madly over his smoking roof. But finally the capricious wind carries the fire away from the little cottage. Policeman Bellinger has won; his house is safe. Only two homes still stand on the North Side—this one and the residence of Mahlon B. Ogden.

News of Chicago's disaster spreads rapidly throughout the nation. Paperboys on the streets of New York City are crying, "Great Fire in Chicago!" . . . "Chicago is Burning Up!" Local businessmen who are visiting in the eastern metropolis frantically attempt to get details about their families. For several hours this morning the New York telegraph office has not been able to establish communication with the stricken city. Word is given out that Western Union in Chicago moved twelve times before the wires went dead. About midafternoon the line is reopened and telegrams are transmitted without charge.

New York City's mayor, Oakley Hall, has just issued a proclamation asking everyone to aid Chicago. Contributions of food and clothing may be taken to the New York Central Station, and according to William Vanderbilt, everything will be transported free of charge. Colonel James Fisk, Jr., is driving a large express wagon through the streets of New York to collect provisions "for the suffering victims of the frightful conflagration."

Help is now coming in from other cities. Mayor Harrison Ludington dispatched three steamers and their crews several hours ago from Milwaukee. They have just arrived, and Chief Williams directs them to points along the north fork of the river where water is accessible. When the steamer *Washington* pulls in from Janesville, Wisconsin, the engine and its fourteen crewmen are assigned to throw water on the North Division's gas storage tanks.

About six o'clock a train from Ohio brings three engines from Cincinnati and one from Dayton. Miles Greenwood, in whose factory the first successful steam-driven fire engine in America was built, is directing the Ohio fire fighters. Chief Williams is gratified that Greenwood has come to help—and says so.

By nightfall there are more than 30,000 refugees crowded into the 230 acres of Lincoln Park. Many have been cowering here all day. And still more homeless come ... some dragging trunks and others carrying small bundles. One young woman has been wandering through the crowds for the past eight hours, a small sack in one hand and three wine glasses clutched between the fingers of her other hand. A fine-looking old gentleman has pulled a half-burned felt hat over his eyes and sits on the grass, gazing listlessly into the frying pan he has managed to salvage. Though darkness has fallen, the park is lighted up "as by a million fire-balloons, sailing over in endless procession."

Will It Never End?

It is 10:30 P.M. when the fire on the North Side begins to subside. John A. Huck, whose residence is located on Fullerton Avenue near the lake shore, has the dubious distinction of owning the last home to burn tonight. Certainly no one can say that the flames have been conquered. There is simply nothing left to burn.

The wind has died down to a gentle breeze, and dark clouds are moving in overhead. Near 11:00 P.M. a cold, drizzling rain begins falling. Chilled though they are, the homeless who are camped on the prairies, on the lake shore, and in Lincoln Park offer silent prayers of gratitude to a Divine Providence.

After burning for more than thirty hours, the fire dies out between 2:00 and 4:00 A.M. on this Tuesday morning, October 10. Surveying the blackened ruins, Chief Williams knows now there is nothing more to be done. He and his men have fought a courageous battle . . . and lost. Taking off his heavy helmet, Williams turns his face upward to feel the refreshing rain. He has had no sleep since the fire began Sunday evening. Now he begins trudging wearily over to the West Side, where his wife has fled.

From Harrison Street on the South Side to Fullerton Avenue on the North Side there is nothing left but debris. The air is heavy with the pungent odor of burned wood, oil, and cloth. The bright flames have died out, but coal piles, still smoking in hundreds of cellars, cast a weird glow. The most disastrous fire in the nation's history has just ended.

13

Smoking Ruins

Tuesday morning, October 10, dawns clear and bright. But the scene in this stricken city is one of appalling devastation. No one knows how many people have perished. Conservatively, the figure is placed between two and three hundred. Almost 100,000 are homeless; some 17,500 buildings have been destroyed.

From an area nearly five miles long and a mile wide, everything has vanished. Joseph Medill speaks of "more widespread, soul-sickening desolation than mortal eye ever beheld . . . ." What was only two days ago a "proud and stately city" is an indescribable chaos of fallen walls and broken columns. Smoke still hovers over the city like a thick black cloud. The streets are covered with debris. Charred trees stand like specters. Here and there gutted walls mark the site of a former brick or stone building, but a thin layer of ashes is all that is left of the wooden structures.

One of the strangest aspects of the fire was its all-consuming heat. A contemporary writer has a theory that the great sheets of flame produced a gas that was carried forward by the wind, penetrating all the buildings in its pathway. Once a blazing brand touched off this gas, the result was instantaneous combustion. Whatever the cause, nothing exposed to the flames has escaped.

Amidst the hundreds of acres left bare this morning, there is not a fragment of charred lumber, not a frame dwelling left anywhere. In the largest downtown buildings the mammoth iron girders expanded upward or downward to such a degree that the walls they supported shattered like falling glass. Even the supposedly fireproof "Athens marble," Chicago's most popular building stone, melted as if it had been placed in a kiln. What were once gas pipes, stoves, scales, and horsecar tracks can no longer be distinguished in their original forms. Instead, fantastic shapes of twisted metal are seen everywhere among the smoking embers. Sheet and pig iron have dissolved into shapeless masses.

Although the ruins of the city water works have not yet cooled, repairs are being started this morning. The engines, it is noted, have been badly mangled. However, the boilers are only slightly damaged. Anyone who is willing, experienced or not, is put to work making steam pipe.

At the corner of State and Randolph streets the fire seems to have made little difference to the chubby apple-woman who always hawks her wares there. Early this morning she trundled her handcart through the debris and set herself up in business. Cheerfully she is calling out, "Apples! Apples! Who'll buy a nice juicy apple?"

Meanwhile, Deacon Bross makes his way through the rubble to the temporary headquarters of the *Chicago Tribune* on Canal Street. Upon arrival, Bross finds that Joseph Medill is already busy with the typesetters, trying to get the machinery ready for the first edition of the *Tribune* tomorrow morning. Noting that both the first floor and the basement must be cleaned up, Bross gets a crew of workmen together, and they clear out the old boards, boxes, and rubbish. His next project is to locate four stoves—a task that requires several hours.

By midafternoon the stoves are in place, and people are already thronging into the office to place advertisements for lost relatives and friends. Bross directs the clerk to take the ads and the cash, marking the transaction carefully in the memorandum book. Using "a dirty old box on the window-sill for a desk," the *Chicago Tribune* is once again doing a lively business.

A few minutes later a man in scorched clothes approaches Mr. Bross, saying, "I haven't a morsel of food for my wife and children tonight and not a cent to buy any; may I paint 'Tribune' over your door?" Bross directs the sign painter to go ahead, and for the modest sum of $3.75 the newspaper establishment is once again identified for all Chicago to see.

Medill and Bross confer on the materials that will be needed to resume publication. They decide that tomorrow Bross should set out for Buffalo and New York to procure the necessary type and paper.

Over on State Street this morning John Mills Van

Osdel, architect for the new Palmer House, returns to the site where the hotel was under construction. Poking through the ruins, he locates the pit where he buried his blueprints. The fire has baked the clay into a solid mass, but probing underneath the architect finds the plans are still intact. Van Osdel is gratified to discover that his insulation has worked so well. He begins to wonder whether clay tile may become a new method for fireproofing.

Along Booksellers' Row the owners of the Western News Company are searching the ruins. Only one small fragment of paper is found—a single leaf from a quarto Bible, charred around the edges. The opening words from the first chapter of the Lamentations of Jeremiah are clearly readable:

> How doth the city sit solitary that was full of people! how is she become as a widow! she that was great among the nations, and princess among the provinces, how is she become tributary! She weepeth sore in the night, and her tears are on her cheeks: among all her lovers she hath none to comfort her.

It is an odd coincidence that just last Sunday the father of one of the Western News clerks took this passage as a text for the sermon in his Connecticut church.

Smoking Ruins

Mayor Mason and the Common Council are meeting today to issue proclamations and orders for the devastated city. The mayor requests all citizens to avoid walking through the burned areas until dangerous walls left standing can be leveled. The price of bread is fixed "at eight cents per loaf of twelve ounces." Furthermore, any drayman or expressman who charges more than the regular fare will have his license revoked. Everyone is warned "to exercise great caution in the use of fire in their dwellings and not to use kerosene lights at present." Those who are willing are asked to report to the corner of Ann and Washington streets "to be sworn in as special policemen." The mayor concludes his final proclamation for the day by requesting all citizens "to aid in preserving the peace, good order and good name of our city."

O. W. Clapp, the merchant whom Mayor Mason appointed yesterday afternoon to distribute relief supplies, has had a busy morning at the Eighteenth Street warehouse. Fifty carloads have arrived, and with the help of volunteers the task of unloading has been completed. Signs have been posted at all the churches, announcing where food, clothing, and shelter will be available.

In Milwaukee Mayor Ludington has directed that a

special train be made up for Chicago relief. On this Tuesday all business in the city is suspended; the schools are closed. Everyone is helping collect supplies for the needy Chicagoans.

Western Union has established headquarters in an old brick warehouse. Boards laid across barrels make temporary desks. And today all telegrams will be sent free of charge. As a result there are long lines of people waiting to inform anxious relatives and friends of their whereabouts.

The railroads are offering free passes to those who wish to leave the city, but most people have decided to stay here—to rebuild both their homes and their businesses.

Chicago citizens, for the most part, are reacting on this first day after the fire with great courage and pluck. Men are saying to each other, "Cheer up; we'll be all right before long." They are pleasant, hopeful, even inclined to be jolly, despite the misery and destitution in which everyone shares.

W. D. Kerfoot is the first individual to get back into active business on this Tuesday morning. He is an energetic real-estate dealer who enlists the assistance of several friends. Hunting up a few pieces of lumber, the little group sets to work at the corner

Smoking Ruins

of State and Washington streets. By noon a small shack has been erected. Tacked to the outside wall is a sign reading:

> W. D. Kerfoot
> 89 Washington St.
> All gone but wife, children, & energy

A painting firm on Madison Street has made temporary arrangements elsewhere. On the ruins of their old establishment they direct their customers as follows:

> MOORE & GOE
> HOUSE and SIGN PAINTERS
> Removed to 111 DesPlaines Ct.,
> Capital, $000,000.30

Over on Clark Street the former Wood's Museum is a mere rubbish heap. The inscription erected here proves that the proprietor has not lost his sense of humor:

> Col. Wood's Museum
> Standing Room Only
> R. Marsh, Treasurer

Relic hunters are everywhere, armed with chisels and hammers. Some are making money by selling souvenirs to strangers and citizens who wish to have a small remembrance of the great fire. One man discovers a group of dolls that have melted and run together. He hawks them as "fire-proof babies."

From the ruins of a store in which paints, oils, and glass were sold, the specimens created by the conflagration have a rare beauty. Masses of glass have been tinted with colors of every hue. The more enterprising are collecting the metals and mailing them to neighboring cities, where they can be converted into souvenir rings and scarf pins.

A story is being circulated around town about the man in East St. Louis who was trying to board a Chicago-bound train last night. Carpetbag in hand, he was pushing and shoving through the crowd. Finally one irritated passenger asked the man why he was in such a hurry. "I must get to Chicago tomorrow," he answered, "or those people up there will have built up the whole town again, and I won't see the ruins."

One of the first residents to return to the city is Mrs. Cyrus McCormick. She was visiting in the East when word came that Chicago was burning. She took the first available train home; when her husband

Smoking Ruins

meets her this afternoon, Mrs. McCormick is dismayed by his appearance. The industrialist is wearing a half-burned coat and slouch hat. Together they make their way through the ruins to the site of his still-smoking factory, where hundreds of employes have gathered, anxious to learn what the boss plans to do.

McCormick is very tempted to sell out now and simply live on the income from his many investments. But his young wife cannot endure the thought that he will not help rebuild the city. She urges him to be a part of the movement she is sure will develop. When he finally agrees and announces his decision to the anxious employes, a loud cheer goes up. He promises to rush orders for lumber and iron; within an hour McCormick is telegraphing his agents to send all the money they can collect from their farmers' accounts. He will need it—and desperately soon.

Another of today's arrivals from New York City is Potter Palmer. He was East on business when news of the fire reached him, and he took the first train home. Now he learns that all his fine new buildings on State Street have burned, that only scant insurance can be paid, that what little income is left will not be sufficient to meet his taxes. Married for only a few months, Mr. Palmer was planning to travel extensively with his bride. He is tempted to sell out now, to leave the community he has helped make great. But like Cyrus McCormick, he asks his wife what he should do.

Without a moment's hesitation, Bertha Honoré Palmer gives her husband an answer. "Mr. Palmer," she says, "it's the duty of every Chicagoan to stay here and help rebuild this stricken city!"

14

"All Is Not Lost"

Over on Canal Street in the *Chicago Tribune*'s temporary office, the first issue since the fire appears on this Wednesday morning, October 11. It is only four pages, poorly printed, but it carries the news that all Chicago is seeking.

On the front page is a five-column story headlined "The Ruins." The ads are primarily "cards" that give new addresses of burned-out firms. The "Lost and Found" column is extensive—pathetic little notices concerning lost mothers, fathers who have become separated from their families, children unable to remember where they lived. Other notices read: "Will the gentleman who gave me the clock and picture on

State st. Oct. 9 call at 258 Cottage Grove—Av. Dr. Steere" . . . "Wanted to find, Swedish girl Sophia, formerly living in my family" . . . "Taken out of the flames, a dark bay mare" . . . these and many, many more tell poignant stories.

Despite all the tragedy, Joseph Medill has written a rousing editorial for this morning's paper entitled "Rebuild the City." In part, he says:

> All is not lost. Though four hundred million dollars worth of property has been destroyed, Chicago still exists. She was not a mere collection of stone, and bricks, and lumber.
>
> These are but the evidence of the power that produced those things . . . the great natural resources are all in existence: the lake, the great outlet from the lakes to the ocean, the thirty-six lines of railway connecting the city with every part of the continent—these, the great arteries of trade and commerce, all remain unimpaired, undiminished and all ready for immediate resumption.
>
> What, therefore, has been lost? We have lost the accumulated profits of twenty years of prosperous growth. We have lost the stock of trade we had on hand the night of the fire. We have lost money—but we have saved life, health, vigor, and industry . . . . Let us avail ourselves of the liberal spirit which the country has shown in our calamity . . . . Let the watchword henceforth be—
> CHICAGO SHALL RISE AGAIN.

"All Is Not Lost"

Even before Medill's stirring words reach his readers, the cleanup process has begun. Truckload after truckload of broken bricks, ashes, and charred rubbish is being hauled to the edge of the lake, to be dumped into the water for landfill. Workmen are busy pulling down shattered walls to clear the way for new buildings.

It is fortunate that the Chicago Relief and Aid Society, a philanthropic group, was organized some ten years ago. Through the efforts of its members, many of the homeless and hungry are being cared for. Makeshift beds have been set up in those churches unharmed by the fire. Doctors and nurses are coming here to treat the sick and injured.

Fire engines are still arriving from other cities today. The companies relieve Chicago firemen, who are badly in need of rest. Without any water supply, and with the weather still extremely dry, it would not take much of a fire to destroy the unburned part of the city. The presence of the out-of-town equipment and men is very reassuring to the citizens. A number of companies, including those from New York City, have promised to remain here for several weeks.

The entire nation is taking Chicago's catastrophe to heart. From all over the country great carloads of provisions are rolling into the city—both food and clothing—which will be distributed through the relief agencies that Mayor Mason has set up. Many of the larger cities are raising funds to send to the homeless refugees.

A Relief Committee from Cincinnati has arrived and is putting up an immense "soup-house" at the rear of the freight depot belonging to the Great Eastern Railroad. It is supervised by Eli Johnson, "as thorough a gentleman as ever made a dish of soup." By tomorrow the kitchen will be ready to distribute 6,000 gallons of soup daily.

"All Is Not Lost"

Throughout the country individuals, too, are making generous contributions to Chicago. The hackmen in Washington, D.C., have voted to turn over a day's fares. Cincinnati newsboys have sent two days' earnings, and the crew of the U.S.S. *Vermont* is giving one day's pay. A personal check for $1,000 has just been received from President Ulysses S. Grant.

Despite this outpouring of goodwill, one unpleasant factor cannot be denied. While the fire was still raging, looting and violence were prevalent in the areas destroyed by flames. One citizen declares that "great consternation and anxiety exists on account of the presence of roughs and thieves." Yesterday Lieutenant General P. H. Sheridan, acting on his own initiative, telegraphed Colonel Nelson A. Miles at Fort Leavenworth for soldiers to reinforce the policemen already on duty in the city. This morning the "boys in blue" arrive—companies of the Fifth United States Infantry Division.

Alarmed citizens have been urging Mayor Mason to put the city under martial law. The mayor has agreed and the following proclamation has just been issued:

> The preservation of the good order and peace of the city is hereby entrusted to the Lieutenant General P. H. Sheridan, U.S. Army.

> The Police will act in conjunction with the Lieut. General in the preservation of the peace and quiet of the city, and the Superintendent of Police will consult with him to that end.
>
> The intent hereof being to preserve the peace of the city, without interfering with the functions of the City Government.

In Springfield, Illinois, the military occupation of Chicago arouses the anger of Governor John M. Palmer. He says that it is illegal and unnecessary. The city should have appealed first to the state government for aid. Nevertheless, the mayor stands firm, and all responsible citizens are rejoicing at the sight of the bluecoats with their glittering muskets. They give "definite assurance of the might of the law."

Now that the ruins are cooled, many safes are being opened in establishments wrecked by fire. Some reveal oddities. A vase of wax flowers is taken from a vault on Dearborn Street and found to be in perfect condition. When Joseph Medill unlocks the safe in the *Chicago Tribune* ruins, he finds the contents in good order. Even the box of matches placed there by one of his reporters is still intact.

There are others not so fortunate, though. James E. McLean, opening his "fireproof vault" in the Customs

"All Is Not Lost"

House, discovers that $1,500,000 in currency for which he is responsible has burned. It will require an Act of Congress to wipe out his staggering debt.

Poking through the debris of the post office building, workmen hear a cheerful meow. They discover the office mascot, a large white-and-brindle cat, squatting in a partially filled pail of water between two burned walls. When the vault is opened at the Fidelity Safe Deposit Insurance Company, the great St. Bernard dog, who serves as a guard, is found alive. These two animals are probably the "only living beings" who have spent the last three days in the fire-swept South Side area.

Deacon Bross, co-publisher of the *Chicago Tribune,* is the first eyewitness of the catastrophe to arrive in New York City. Immediately he is front-page news. To the reporters he gives vivid accounts of people standing by heaps of ashes and planning how to rebuild Chicago. What a splendid opportunity, he says, for eastern brains and money to help in the work and share the profits that will be inevitable.

Not only does Bross talk with newspapermen, but he also accepts every invitation to make a speech— even climbs on a soapbox in the street to talk where a crowd has gathered, urging everyone to come to his town. "Within five years," he predicts, "Chicago's business houses will be rebuilt and by the year 1900 the new Chicago will boast a population of a million people . . . what Chicago has been in the past, she must become in the future and a hundred fold more."

Yesterday John B. Drake, owner of the demolished Tremont House, discovered in walking around the charred ruins that the Michigan Avenue Hotel was still standing. Excited by the fact that he had a signed contract to purchase this hotel, Drake wired to New

York for a large loan. This morning he walks into the hotel with cash in hand. The proprietor, knowing this is the only hostelry still standing in town, refuses to sell and says there is no law that can make him.

Drake turns on his heel and leaves, returning a few moments later with four friends. He places his watch on the hotel desk, advising the present owner that he has five minutes to deliver the property. Drake's friends make several loud remarks about how close Lake Michigan is, how easy it would be to throw the hesitant proprietor into the water and watch him flounder. This conversation settles the issue; the sale is completed. John B. Drake is now the new owner, and he renames the hotel—The Tremont House.

Once the smoke clears away, it is found that in addition to personal belongings, some thousands of loads of merchandise have been saved, merchandise "stowed away in tunnels, buried in back alleys, piled up all along the lake shore, strewn in front yards through the avenues, run out of the city in box cars, and even, in some instances, freighted upon the decks of schooners off the harbor." With such a backlog of saleable items, temporary stores are immediately set up in houses on the South Side, well beyond the ruins.

Says one contemporary writer, "The carelessness,

even recklessness, with which Commerce has dropped down into dwelling houses, haphazard, is grotesque and whimsical to the last degree." Under a single roof there may be as many as three or four businesses. One home has a shoe store in the basement, a button factory on the first floor, doctors' and lawyers' offices scattered through the second floor, and a telegraph office in the attic.

The residence of a bank president has become a shop for feminine finery; a small artist's cottage is converted into a grocery where "barrels of molasses and vinegar and flour lie impudently and lazily in the yard." A watch factory has set up operations in an abandoned church, while an express office has taken space in another church.

The merchant Marshall Field, confident of Chicago's future, is making his plans with considerably more foresight. This morning ends what has been a two-day search for a suitable place in which to resume business. Field has just leased a two-story red brick barn at State and Twentieth streets, a building in which the Chicago City Railway Company formerly quartered horses. While his partner, Levi Leiter, makes an inventory of the goods that have been saved, Marshall Field gets a crew of workmen together and directs activities at the barn.

The oat bins and stacks of hay can be pitched out, he says; the harnesses, reins, and blinders stored in another building. Once the cleanup process is completed, the floors will be varnished and the walls whitewashed. Pine counters can be constructed and moved in to replace the horse stalls. Field's credit is good; fresh merchandise can be rushed in from New York. Within three weeks the merchant estimates that he will once again be ready to serve the elegant "carriage trade" of Chicago.

Businessmen returning to Chicago these past two days report that they have not found a solemn face among their friends. With fortunes completely gone, these men are starting to rebuild from the smoldering rubble. Energy, experience, reputation—these are the qualities possessed by leading citizens; the credit needed is quickly being extended by New York bankers. Everyone is saying, "What we have done before, we can do again."

The men who have made Chicago great are undaunted in their faith. Already plans are in the making for new structures, finer than those that have burned. Possessed with tremendous courage, these men are confident that a new and better city will arise from the ruins.

15

"Chicago Shall Rise Again"

Some eighty days have passed since the Great Chicago Fire finally burned itself out. It is now December 31, 1871. Tomorrow brings a new year, and with it new hope for the future. Contributions have been extremely generous; nearly $5,000,000 has been received—more than $900,000 coming from foreign donors.

For those who were homeless, thousands of tents and barracks were erected, although these temporary dwellings also brought health problems. Without stoves the residents were unable to boil water. The result was a rash of typhoid fever cases. However, by the end of November repairs were completed in the city's water works. All pumps began working at full capacity, and pure water was once again available to Chicagoans.

Fortunately, the weather has been good, and rebuilding is continuing at a brisk pace. Farmers, once their harvests were finished, flocked into town from as far as 150 miles away to take temporary jobs. Laborers, carpenters, and bricklayers are receiving higher wages than ever before; "everywhere is heard the clink of trowel and the stroke of hammer."

One contemporary writer says:

> If anyone thinks Chicago has lost her population, and with it her enterprise, he should stand on Madison, Randolph, or Lake Street bridges at dusk and watch the myriads of laborers and mechanics that, having finished their day's work in the ruins, crowd over those structures to their homes in the West Division. So innumerable are they, they seem to rise from brick heaps like coveys of wild fowl.

Inflation, however, has caught Chicago in its tentacles. A small house that would have rented for $12 a month before the fire is eagerly snatched up now for

$75. Some grocers have doubled the price of meat and sugar; even then the stock is quickly bought up. Not all merchants are trying to make money, though. A West Side grocer hangs a sign on his window that reads, "All Parties Without Money Can Have Meat Here."

Plans are now being made to build the city's first public library—a project inspired by a donation received from England. It was suggested by Thomas Hughes, author of *Tom Brown at Rugby,* that the people of England should give books to the wrecked city. Queen Victoria, as well as Tennyson, Browning, Darwin, Kingsley, and many others have sent a total of some 8,000 volumes.

Out at Field & Leiter's horse barn, business is booming. Clerks helped spruce up the new store. Merchandise from New York arrived in such quantities that bobtail horsecars were used to haul it to the new location. One evening a policeman stopped to ask the drayman where he was taking such a large load. Told that it was going out to the renovated horse barn, the policeman shook his head in wonder. "That beats all," he said. "Seems that there's nothing impossible at Field & Leiter's."

On October 21 the partners ran an ad on the front page of the *Chicago Tribune* announcing that within a

"Chicago Shall Rise Again"

few days they would open a complete retail store. In conclusion the ad read, "We sincerely thank our friends for their many kind expressions of sympathy and hope soon to renew our former pleasant business relations."

The horse barn, of course, has none of the elegance of the Field & Leiter marble palace that was lost in the flames. But the merchandise is still of the same fine quality—linens, laces, shawls, cloaks, all the latest fashions from New York. Marshall Field stands at the door, as of old, to greet the ladies and give them any needed assistance. Department chiefs are easily identified by the carnations in their lapels; salesmen are as neatly dressed, as courteous, as ever.

A reporter records the scene: "Here are hundreds of clerks and thousands of patrons a day, busy along the spacious aisles and the vast vistas of ribbons and laces and cloaks and dress goods. This tells no story of a fire. The ladies jostle each other as impatiently as of old . . . ."

Another powerful man on the Chicago scene is Potter Palmer. He has moved swiftly these past three months with plans for even finer buildings on State Street than those he lost. Because of his excellent credit record, he has been able to borrow $1,700,000 from the Connecticut Mutual Life Insurance Company—the "largest single loan made in the United States" up to this time. Added to this is another $1,000,000 which he has obtained from mortgages.

A new Palmer House is under construction. So anxious is the owner to have it finished that artificial lights have been put up in order for workmen to continue night and day—something no one has ever thought of doing before. Because of Potter Palmer's obvious confidence in the city's future, other prominent men are following his lead.

By October 23 it was felt that sufficient order had been restored in the city for the civil authorities to resume control. The military troops left town the following day. However, it was not long before an undercurrent of fear began to develop. A committee of prominent citizens called on the mayor and asked him to have the infantry returned. Despite the protests of Governor Palmer and the state legislature, the troops will now remain until after the first of next month. There has been a decided drop in serious crimes; the presence of the military men, it is felt, provides "the breathing spell that the city needs to recover its courage and confidence."

A depot has been established at the Central Police Station for unclaimed goods. Some have been brought in voluntarily, but many have been ferreted out by the police. There is an endless variety here: trunks, bureaus, carpets, oil paintings, clocks, silverware, shoes, guns, and books. By mid-November the depot contained nearly $1,000,000 worth of property. Ultimately it will all be restored to the rightful owners.

Late last month a two-week inquiry was held by the Board of Police and Fire Commissioners. Its primary purpose was to establish the cause of the fire and to evaluate the work of the Fire Department.

Someone had started a rumor that Kate O'Leary had taken a kerosene lamp into the barn and was milking one of her cows on that fatal Sunday evening. Supposedly, the cow had kicked over the lamp and the barn had immediately caught fire. Reporters snatched up this rumor and enlarged it, until the entire nation was blaming the poor Irish woman and her famous animal. However, the board's report makes no such statement. It is probable that the cause of Chicago's great holocaust will forever remain a mystery.

During the inquiry no criticism was made of Chief Marshal Robert Williams. In studying the progress of the fire, the board found that the chief had done everything possible. Once the flames surged across the river, he had left enough engines on the West Side to control the blaze there, but had moved the greater part of his forces to the South Side as quickly as it was feasible to get orders to the officers in charge. After the water works was gone, there was very little fire fighting that could be done except in limited areas along the river.

There are many who feel that the blame for the catastrophe should be placed on the city government. They say that the Common Council failed to do its duty. For instance, Mayor Mason and his aldermen knew very well that the city was a tinderbox, that construction of buildings was extremely poor. They were too penny-pinching in their allotments to provide a fire department that was adequately manned and sufficiently equipped to cope with a great fire. Furthermore, they failed to enact a building code that would eliminate fire hazards and faulty construction.

Hopefully, all that will now be changed. The month of November brought a municipal election. Everyone felt that personal honesty, above everything else, was needed. The leading political parties met together and decided on a nonpartisan ticket, the "Union-Fireproof." Republican Joseph Medill was persuaded to head the ticket as mayor, though he accepted the job very reluctantly, writing a friend that the powers of the office were so restricted they left him "but the shadow of authority with all the responsibility that falls on the office." The professional politicians who opposed the nonpartisan idea were called "irresponsible soreheads" by the *Chicago Tribune.* But the Medill ticket was swept into office by an overwhelming majority.

In his inaugural message the new mayor spoke firmly:

> The outside walls of every building hereafter erected within the limits of Chicago should be composed of materials as incombustible as brick, stone, concrete or slate . . . I recommend that your honorable body proceed to frame and perfect a fire ordinance that will give security and permanence to the future city.

Epilogue: 1875

During the first few weeks after the fire, thousands of temporary buildings sprang up. Constructed of wood, these shanties caused a *Tribune* editor to observe that they were "as dangerous as powder kegs."

Other hazards were noticeable. Brick structures, so-called, were often made of wood except for the exterior walls. The popular "mansard roofs" of supposedly fireproof materials sometimes proved to be merely pine, covered with tin or slate.

Soon after Mayor Joseph Medill took office, the Common Council passed an ordinance fixing the "fire limits" of the city. These limits included all of the business district on the South Side, the residential area on the North Side up to Fullerton Avenue, and about half of the industrial West Side. Within the boundaries established, wooden buildings were absolutely prohibited. Elaborate standards were set up for interior construction of large buildings—all, of course, with a view toward safety.

Unfortunately, the municipal authorities who were appointed to investigate new construction were not reliable. Their inspections became something of a farce; bribery was not uncommon. Many structures, which supposedly were adhering to the new building code, had roofs "as inflammable as a pile of kindling."

Throughout his term of office Joseph Medill tried very hard to enforce the new fire regulations, but his efforts were not successful. In the election of 1873 Medill was ousted, and Harvey D. Colvin became mayor. All restrictions were promptly forgotten.

Just how dangerous this apathy could be was demonstrated in July 1874, when fire once again struck Chicago. Sixty acres south and west of Van Buren Street and Michigan Avenue were wiped out. Insurance underwriters threatened to withdraw from the city unless some drastic corrective steps were taken.

Indignant businessmen formed a Citizens' Association and brought pressure to bear on the Common Council. More fire-fighting equipment was purchased; more men were added to the force. And the fire limits

Epilogue: 1875

were extended to coincide with the boundaries of the city. Just a few weeks ago the council created a new Executive Department whose sole purpose will be to survey and inspect buildings. It is now hoped that the regulations will be more rigidly enforced.

Despite all the recent furor, there are many who say that the conflagration of 1871 was actually a blessing, that Chicago was "set forward ten years" by the fire. For the most part the new homes and churches, schools and theaters, retail stores and hotels, newspaper establishments and factories, are a vast improvement over the old.

An English visitor to the city recently observed: "The business streets are lined with handsome, massive houses, some six and seven stories high, substantially built, sometimes of red brick with stone copings and elaborate carving, while others are of that creamy stone which reminds one of the Paris boulevards."

There is great promise for the years ahead. The men of vision who guided the destinies of the city before the Great Fire are again hard at work. Though their loss of material possessions was overwhelming, the courage of these leaders has not faltered. By their example they leave to future generations a legacy that is priceless—the indomitable Chicago Spirit!

Bibliography

Books

* *Indicates books that are readily available and may be of special interest to the readers of this book.*

Andreas, A. T. *History of Chicago.* Vol. II. Chicago: A. T. Andreas Company, 1885

* Angle, Paul M., comp. *The Great Chicago Fire Described in Seven Letters by Men and Women Who Experienced Its Horrors, and Now Published in Commemoration of the Seventy-fifth Anniversary of the Catastrophe.* Chicago: The Chicago Historical Society, 1946

Barclay, George Lippard. *The Great Fire of Chicago.* Chicago: Philip Barclay & Co., 1872

Casson, Herbert N. *Cyrus Hall McCormick.* Chicago: A. C. McClurg & Co., 1909

Chicago Board of Public Works, Eleventh Annual Report. Chicago: D. and C. H. Blakely, 1872

Bibliography

Chicago Relief and Aid Society, Report of, to the Common Council. Chicago: Horton and Leonard, 1872

Chicago Times. New Chicago: A Full Review of the Work of Reconstruction. Articles from the paper preserved in the Chicago Historical Society

Colbert, Elias, and Chamberlin, Everett. *Chicago and the Great Conflagration.* Cincinnati and New York: C. F. Vent, 1872

* Cook, Frederick. *Bygone Days in Chicago.* Chicago: A. C. McClurg & Co., 1910

* Cromie, Robert. *The Great Chicago Fire.* New York: McGraw-Hill Book Company, 1958

* Dedmon, Emmett. *Fabulous Chicago.* New York: Random House, 1953

Goodspeed, E. J. *History of the Great Fires in Chicago and the West.* New York: H. S. Goodspeed & Co., 1871

* Graham, Jory. *Chicago: An Extraordinary Guide.* Chicago: Rand McNally & Company, 1967

* Hansen, Harry. *The Chicago.* New York: Rinehart & Co., Inc., 1942

Hayes, Dorsha B. *Chicago: Crossroads of American Enterprise.* New York: Julian Messner, Inc., 1944

Kinsley, Philip. *The* Chicago Tribune: *Its First Hundred Years.* Vol. II. Chicago: The Tribune Company, 1945

* Lewis, Lloyd. *Chicago: The History of its Reputation.* New York: Harcourt, Brace & Company, 1929

Luzerne, Frank. *The Lost City.* New York: Wells & Co., 1872

Mackintosh, Charles H. *The Doomed City.* Detroit: Michigan News, 1871

Masters, Edgar Lee. *The Tale of Chicago.* New York: G. P. Putnam's Sons, 1933

McDonald, R. *Illustrated History and Map of Chicago with History of the Great Fire.* New York: R. B. Thompson, 1872

* McIlvaine, Mable. *Reminiscences of Chicago During the Great Fire.* Chicago: The Lakeside Press, 1915

McKenna, John J. *Reminiscences of the Chicago Fire.* Chicago: Clobesey & Co., 1933

* Morris, John V. *Fires and Firefighters.* New York: Bramhall House, 1953

Musham, H. A. "The Great Chicago Fire." *Papers in Illinois History,* pp. 69–189. Springfield, Ill.: The Illinois State Historical Society, 1941

Peterson, Virgil W. *Barbarians in Our Midst: A History of Chicago Crime and Politics.* Boston: Little Brown & Co., 1952

Pierce, Bessie Louise. *A History of Chicago.* Vol. III. New York: Alfred A. Knopf, 1957

* Poole, Ernest. *Giants Gone: Men Who Made Chicago.* New York: McGraw-Hill Book Company, 1943

Bibliography

Randall, Frank A. *History of the Development of Building Construction in Chicago.* Urbana, Ill.: University of Illinois Press, 1949

* Ross, Ishbel. *Silhouette in Diamonds: The Life of Mrs. Potter Palmer.* New York: Harper & Brothers, 1960

Sheahan, James W. *The Great Conflagration.* Chicago: Union Publishing Company, 1871

Strickland, A. *The Chicago Fire, October 8th and 9th, 1871.* Chicago: Brown and Colbert, 1871

* Tebbel, John. *An American Dynasty: The Story of the McCormicks, Medills and Pattersons.* Garden City, N.Y.: Doubleday & Company, 1947

* Wagenknecht, Edward. *Chicago.* Norman, Okla.: University of Oklahoma Press, 1964

* Wendt, Lloyd, and Kogan, Herman. *Give the Lady What She Wants: The Story of Marshall Field & Company.* Chicago: Rand McNally & Company, 1952

Wilkie, F. B. *Walks About Chicago, 1871–1881.* Chicago: Belford, Clarke & Co., 1880

Letters, Scrapbooks, and Privately Printed Manuscripts

Blatchford, Mary Emily. *Memories of the Chicago Fire.* Privately printed by Mr. and Mrs. Paul Blatchford for the benefit of the Chicago Historical Society, October 1921

Burgess, O. A. *The Late Chicago Fire.* Photostatic copy presented to the Chicago Historical Society

Deane, Charles, comp. *Scrapbook of Clippings Regarding the Chicago Fire, 1871.* Chicago Historical Society

Foster, Thomas Dove. *A Letter from the Fire: An Account of the Great Chicago Fire Written in 1871.* Privately printed. Cedar Rapids, Iowa: Torch Press, 1949

Hubbard, Mary Ann. *Family Memories.* Printed for private circulation, 1912

Hutchinson, W. A. *Some Recollections of the Chicago Fire.* Typewritten manuscript in the Chicago Historical Society

Loesch, Frank Joseph. *Personal Experiences During the Chicago Fire, 1871.* Chicago: Privately printed, 1925

McLaury, Cornelia. *Recollections of the Chicago Fire.* Manuscript presented to the Chicago Historical Society, 1929

Scrapbook of clippings relating to the Chicago Fire, 1871. The Chicago Historical Society

Newspaper files for 1871 of *Chicago Times; Chicago Evening Journal; Chicago Tribune; The New York Times; Washington Evening Star*

Index

Allen-Mackey Carpet Co., 113
Arnold, Isaac N., 107, 136, 137
Associated Press, 76
Audubon Club, 28-29

Bateham, W. B., 50-51
Bellinger, Richard, 139-140
Benner, Matthias, 19, 24
Booksellers' Row, 28, 60, 90-91, 150
Boyer, Andrew, 64-65
Brinks Express Co., 91
Bross, Deacon, 78, 79, 96, 122-123, 128, 148-149
  in New York, 164

Brown (fire engine), 126-127
buildings, 4, 5-6, 7, 11, 28, 134, 143, 159
  and building codes, 19, 175, 176, 177-178, 179
  evacuation of, 20-21, 51, 74-75, 76, 77, 81, 82-84, 86-88, 117, 119-120, 122
  explosion of, for firebreaks, 44, 55, 68-69, 114-115, 139
  fireproofing of, 29, 60-61, 78-79, 94, 97-98, 99, 122, 148, 150, 162-163, 176, 177
O'Leary barn, 34-36, 37-40, 41, 43, 46, 55, 174

buildings (*cont.*)
  rents, 169-170
  slum, 33-34, 62, 63-64
  temporary, 168-169, 177
  wetting-down, 50, 53, 55, 71, 94, 99, 114, 139-140
Bullwinkle, Benjamin, 18, 55

Canal St., 19, 23, 40, 46, 47-48, 51
Carson, Pirie, Scott and Co., 60
Chapin, John R., 77
Chicago (fire engine), 41, 44, 73
Chicago, Past, Present and Future (Wright), 127-128
Chicago Academy of Design, 28, 117-118
Chicago Academy of Sciences, 28-29
Chicago Board of Police, 15, 174
Chicago Board of Trade, 132-133
Chicago City Railway Co., 166
Chicago Club, 125-126
Chicago Courthouse, 18, 26, 68
  fire of, 72, 73-76, 77, 80
  watchmen in, 41-42, 45-46, 61-62
Chicago *Evening Journal* (newspaper), 130-131
Chicago Fire (1871):
  estimated losses, 145
  first alarm, 14, 19
  investigation of causes, 174-176
  last building burned, 143
  prevention methods after, 176-179
Chicago Fire (1874), 178-179
Chicago Fire Dept., 14-24, 31-32, 109, 114, 132
  alarm system, 17-18, 20, 26, 40, 42, 43, 61-62, 71, 74, 76
  DeKoven St. fire and, 40-45, 46-47, 174-175
  engines, 15-16, 17, 24, 56, 57-58, 63, 126-127, 128, 159
  See also Williams, Chief Marshal Robert A.
Chicago Health Dept., 132
Chicago Historical Society, 29-30, 97-98
Chicago Insurance Patrol, 18, 55
Chicago River, 9, 23, 60, 80, 81, 82
  bridges on, 4-5, 21, 43, 52, 55, 63, 64-65, 77, 88-89, 93, 137
  forks of, 2, 3
  relief station on, 133
  vessels on, 92-94, 136-138
  waterworks pumping station on, 11, 13
Chicago Soldiers' Home, 30
Chicago Times (newspaper), 92
Chicago Tribune (newspaper), 26-27, 33, 51-52, 164, 176

Index

Chicago Tribune (cont.)
  on Field and Leiter's, 70, 170-171
  reopening of, 148-149, 157-159, 162
  South Side fire and, 78-80, 94-96, 110, 119-121, 122, 129-131
Chicago White Stockings, 30, 112, 124
Cincinnati, Ohio, 56, 141, 160, 161
Citizens' Association, 178-179
Clapp, O. W., 132-133, 151
Clark St., 74, 76, 100, 137, 153
Clifford (tugboat), 136-138
Colbert, Elias, 79, 120
Colvin, Harvey D., 178
Common Council, 11, 13, 151
  budgeting of, 15, 16, 18, 175, 178-179
Conley's Patch, 62, 63-64, 66
Connecticut Mutual Life Insurance Co., 171-172
Corkran, William, 97-98
County Jail, 61, 74-75
Coventry (fire engine), 49-50
Crosby's Opera House, 32-33, 112
Customs House, 162-163

Dayton, Ohio, 141
Dearborn St., 29, 66, 86, 97, 112
  architecture of, 60-61
  newspaper offices on, 78, 92, 119
DeKoven St., 34-36, 37-42, 129
Democratic Press (newspaper), 78
Drake, John B., 86-87, 126-127, 164-165
drought, 10, 26

Election of 1871, 175-176
Election of 1873, 178
Emancipation Proclamation, 29-30, 98
English, G. P., 51-52, 79

Farwell Hall, 1-2, 9-10, 14, 110
Fidelity Safe Deposit Insurance Co., 163-164
Field, Marshall, 69-70, 113, 116, 166-167, 171
Field & Leiter's Store, 60, 69-70, 91, 113-114, 116
  reopening, 166-167, 170-171
"Fire limits" ordinance, 177-178, 179
food, 70, 151, 160
Fort Dearborn, 8
Fort Leavenworth, Kans., 161
Fort Wayne railroad, 68

Galena and Chicago Union Railroad, 9
Gas Works, 47, 53, 62-63, 79, 141
Goll, Bruno, 40, 42

Grand Pacific Hotel, 85-86
Great Eastern Railroad, 160
Greenwood, Miles, 141
Gund (fire engine), 53, 63

Hall, Oakley, 140-141
Hannis, Alonzo, 66, 68, 110
Hildreth, James H., 44, 55, 68-69, 114-115, 139
Horton, D. H., 128-129
Huck, John A., 143

Illinois Central Railway, 56, 92

Janesville, Wis., 141
Johnson, Eli, 160
Joliet, Ill., 6

Kaufman, Sergeant, 56-57
Kerfoot, W. D., 152-153

Lagger, Joseph, 40-41
Lake Michigan, 2, 8, 13, 60, 91, 92, 113, 158, 159
   beaches of, 104-107, 111, 113-114, 115, 126, 128, 143
   pumping from, 99-100, 126-127, 128
Lake St., 55, 77, 86, 116, 124
Lee, William, 40, 42
Leiter, Levi, 69-70, 113, 116
Liberty (fire engine), 24
Lighthouse Pier, 107, 136
lighting, 32, 47, 63, 79, 87, 95, 103, 151

Lincoln, Abraham, 29-30, 33, 61, 86, 107, 131
   funeral train of, 125
Lincoln Park, 104, 130, 139, 143
Little Giant (fire engine), 16, 19, 40, 41-42
Long John (fire engine), 16, 47, 58
looting, 64, 70, 75, 84, 87-88, 90, 123
   martial law and, 161-162
   Pinkerton agency and, 131-132
Ludington, Harrison, 56, 141, 151-152

McCagg mansion, 100
McCormick, Cyrus Hall, 135-136, 155
McCormick, Mrs. Cyrus Hall, 154-155
McCormick Harvester Works, 135
McLaughlin, Patrick, 34, 35
McLean, James E., 162-163
McVicker's Theatre, 119, 121
Mandel Brothers Store, 114
Mason, Roswell B., 56, 68, 74, 115, 132, 175
   martial law and, 161-162
   relief measures of, 151, 159
Medill, Joseph, 78, 79, 94-96, 119-121, 122, 145
   as mayor, 176, 177-178

Index

Medill, Joseph (*cont.*)
   Tribune reopening by, 148-149, 158-159, 162
Medill, Samuel, 51-52, 78, 79
Merchants' Insurance building, 76
Michigan Ave., 60, 91, 111, 122-124, 125-126, 178
Michigan Ave. Hotel, 126-127, 164-165
Milwaukee, Wis., 56, 138, 141, 151-152
Moody, Dwight L., 82
Moore & Goe, firm, 153
Mutual Security Insurance Company, 27

National (Baseball) Association, 30
National Elevator, 24
New York Central Railroad, 125, 141
New York City, 115, 116, 167, 170
   fire engine loan, 56, 159
   relief aid from, 140-141, 164
Noble, Charles, 93-94
North Side, 2-3, 5, 29, 52, 53, 65, 177
   fire in, 80-84, 97-108, 130, 134-144
   gas transfer to, 47, 63, 141
   prisoner transfer to, 74
   waterworks, 11, 99-100
Northwestern Railroad, 66, 80

Ockerby, Thomas, 47, 53, 63
Ogden, Mahlon B., 100-101, 140
O'Leary, Patrick and Kate, DeKoven St. fire and, 34-36, 37-40, 41, 42, 43, 46, 55, 129, 174

Palmer, Bertha Honoré (Mrs. Potter Palmer), 117, 155-156
Palmer, Governor John M., 162, 173
Palmer, Potter, 60, 69, 115-117, 155-156, 171-172
Palmer House, 60, 115-119, 150, 172
Parmalee, Franklin, 53-55
Parmalee Omnibus and Stage Company, 54-55, 62
Pinkerton, Allan, 131-132
Pioneer, The (railroad car), 124
Post Office, 66, 68, 109-110
Pullman, George M., 7, 124-125
Pullman Palace Car Company, 125

Quirk, Daniel W., 23

railroads, 3, 5, 7, 8, 9, 112, 154, 158
   baggage vans, 53-54
   engine shipment by, 56
   fire on, 21-22, 80, 92
   mail and, 68
   refugee passes on, 152

railroads (*cont.*)
  relief trains, 133, 141, 151-152, 159-160
  sleeping cars, 124-125
rainfall, 10-11, 26, 143
Randolph St., 27, 42-43, 74, 77, 111, 148
refugees, 93, 115, 145, 161, 168
  North Side, 82-84, 100-108, 136, 139, 141-143
  relief facilities for, 132-133, 141, 142-143, 151-152, 159-160
  South Side, 64, 74-75, 80, 86-90, 110-112, 122-123, 126
  tugboat rescue operation, 136-138
  West Side, 51, 52
Republican Party, 78, 176
Rhem (fire engine), 49-50
Rice (fire engine), 126-127

St. Paul's Catholic Church, 48, 49-51
Sands, the, 104-107
Sanitary Fair (1863), 29
Schafer, Mathias, 41-42, 46, 74
Second National Bank, 65-66, 82
Sheridan, Lt.-Gen. P. H., 161-162
Sherman House, 76-77
South Side, 2, 3-4, 5, 42, 46, 47, 51, 52, 62, 111
  animal survivors, 163-164
  fire on, 58, 59-72, 73-80, 83, 85-96, 109-121, 122-130, 134, 136, 143, 175
Springfield, Ill., 125, 131, 162
Stanton, Edwin M., quoted, 135
State St., 28, 110, 116-119, 148, 149-150
  bridge at, 137, 138
  stores on, 60, 69-70, 113, 116, 166
Stone, Col. Samuel, 97-98
Sullivan, Danny "Peg-leg," 35-36, 37-38
Swing, Rev. David, 83-84

Terrace Row, 60, 122, 126, 127, 128
Thomas, Theodore, 33, 112
Tinkham, Edward Isley, 65-66, 82-83, 107
  tugboat trip of, 136-138
Titsworth (fire engine), 47
Train, George Francis, 1-2, 9-10, 110
Tremont House, 8, 86-87, 126, 127, 164-165
tunnels, 5, 87
typhoid fever, 169

Union-Fireproof Party, 176
Union National Bank, 68
Union Pacific Railroad, 3, 9
United States Weather Bureau, 25-26, 56-57, 112-113

Van Osdel, John Mills, 118-119, 149-150
volunteer fire companies, 14-15

Index

Wabash Ave., 53, 60, 91, 110, 115, 127
wagons, 82, 83, 90-91, 113-114, 122-123, 141, 151
Walters, Lorens, 19
water, 126-127, 128, 168-169
  mains, 18, 100
  rooftop tanks, 94
  supply stoppage, 109, 110, 114, 120, 140, 159
Washington (fire engine), 141
Washington, D.C., 131, 161
Washington Square, 27, 100
Washington St., 68, 70, 111, 115, 132, 151
  tunnel, 5, 87
Water Works, 11, 13, 99-100, 148, 175
Waubansia (fire engine), 16, 47
Wentworth, John, 16
Western News Co., 150
Western Union Telegraph Co., 76, 140, 152
West Side, 2, 4, 169, 177
  bridges, 65
  first fire (October 7), 14, 19-24, 25-26, 31-32, 33, 42, 52, 63
  second fire (DeKoven St.), 36, 37-48, 49-58, 63, 128, 130, 136, 174-175
Wilkie, Franc B., quoted, 13
William James (fire engine), 24
Williams, Chief Marshal Robert A., 18, 19-21, 31-32
  North Side fire and, 99-100, 141, 143
  South Side fire and, 58, 60, 61, 62, 63, 68, 69, 80, 109, 114, 128, 175
  West Side second fire and, 42-45, 47, 48, 51, 56-58, 129, 175
wood, 4, 5, 9, 11, 19
  bridge construction in, 65-66, 137, 138
  fencing with, 33, 81, 84, 139
  "fire limits" ordinance on, 177-178
  paving uses of, 8, 55, 81, 84, 90, 98, 108, 116, 139
Wood's Museum, 29, 110, 153
Wright, John S., 127-128
Wright's Stables, 80-81, 82

Young's Horsecar Line, 91

ABOUT THE AUTHOR

Having lived and worked in Chicago for several years, Mary Kay Phelan is especially interested in the city's history—particularly the Great Fire of 1871.

American history has been both a vocation and an avocation for Mrs. Phelan. With her husband she is involved in the production of 8-millimeter films that are widely used in schools and libraries. She is the author of *Four Days in Philadelphia—1776*, which tells the story of the adoption of the Declaration of Independence; *Midnight Alarm*, an account of Paul Revere's ride; a biography of Dr. Florence Sabin; and three books in the Crowell Holiday series: *Mother's Day, The Fourth of July,* and *Election Day.* Mrs. Phelan was born in Baldwin City, Kansas, was graduated from DePauw University in Indiana, and received her M.A. from Northwestern University. She lives with her family in Davenport, Iowa.

ABOUT THE ILLUSTRATOR

William Plummer grew up in Philadelphia and was graduated from the Philadelphia College of Art, where he later taught drawing, advertising art, and illustrating. He has also studied at the Brighton School of Art in England, and has traveled in Great Britain and many parts of Europe, including Germany, France, and Czechoslovakia. His fondness for travel and for history is reflected in his art.

Mr. Plummer's works have been exhibited in museums and galleries in Philadelphia and New York.

Mr. Plummer, with his wife and two children, lives in Pennsylvania.